CALLED TO CHINA

**Attie Bostick's Life and Missionary Letters
From China: 1900-1943**

Copyright © 2006
Rebekah E. Adams

All rights reserved.
Written permission must be secured from the publisher
to use or reproduce any part of this book,
except for brief quotations in articles or reviews.

Printed in the United States of America
Library of Congress Control Number: 2006906964
ISBN: 0-9788311-0-1

Book Design by Jason Hodges
Edited by Keith E. Durso

SAN: >>>>>>>>   851-7460   <<<<<<<<<<

Halldale Publishing Company
P.O. Box 4247
Huntsville, AL 35815

To my mother

Rebekah Putnam Ellis

and

my daughter

Reverend M. Amanda Adams

Contents

Preface vii

Prologue 1

Chapter One:
Attie Bostick's Family 7

Chapter Two:
Attie's Years with the Gospel Mission Program, 1900–1915 23

Chapter Three:
Attie's First Years as a Southern Baptist Missionary, 1916–1921 39

Chapter Four:
Attie's Ministry During Political Unrest, 1922–1929 55

Chapter Five:
Attie's "Patch Work," 1930–1938 77

Chapter Six:
Attie's Ministry During the Japanese Occupation of China, 1938–1941 ... 97

Chapter Seven:
Attie's Years of Internment, 1941–1943 115

Epilogue 133

Appendix 136

Index 141

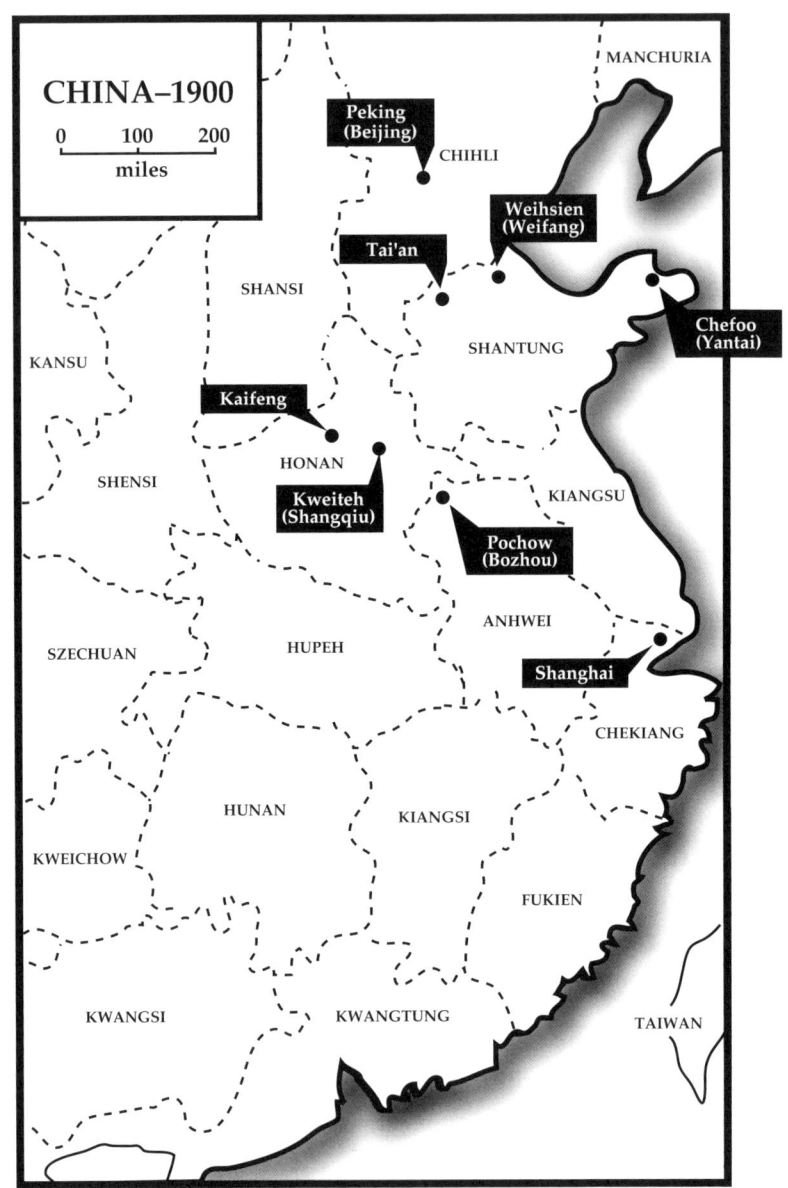

Preface

I met my great-aunt Attie Texas Bostick League at her home in Forest City, North Carolina, when I was a child in the late 1950s. My mother, Rebekah Putnam Ellis, always admired Attie and her work as a Southern Baptist missionary to China, and would take my younger brother Tim and me to visit Attie and her niece Bertha Bostick. On one visit, Attie gave me a six-inch, wedge-shaped, red-embroidered shoe that she told me an eighty-year-old Chinese woman had worn. Attie was in her eighties then, with her years in China long past. I never heard her talk about her missionary work, and she did not describe her work in China to extended family in her later years.

As the family historian, my mother received numerous Bostick family pictures and many of the letters Attie had sent from China during her ministry there from 1900 to 1943. The pictures and letters remained unnoticed for years until the summer of 2004 when a change in my work schedule provided the time for me to examine the numerous letters and pictures of Attie and her brothers George Pleasant (G. P.) and Wade, who also served as missionaries to China. Also in 2004, my daughter, Mary Amanda Adams, was entering her final year at Princeton Theological Seminary, where she was studying to become a Presbyterian minister, and my niece, Hannah Clarke, a missions major at Ambassador College in Lattimore, North Carolina, traveled to Brazil on a mission trip during which she worked with the deaf. That summer, I decided that I needed to research the lives of our family members, particularly Attie, who had been missionaries to China.

As I typed Attie's flowing but almost undecipherable hand-written letters, I discovered the fascinating story of a woman of incredible determination who became a missionary to China despite the prevailing societal pressures for her to marry for protection and security. The way she dealt with the uncertainty of the financial support of her ministry and her accounts of the famines and bandit attacks in China were inspiring. When she was interned by the Japanese and was erroneously told numerous times that she would be allowed to return to the United States to her family, she relied on her faith in God to give her the strength to endure.

After reading about Attie's faith and service in a distant land, I became convinced that her story was too important and too inspirational to remain buried in folders that have unfortunately been labeled with her married name. Late in life, Attie married T. J. League, but most people who knew her, and her family members who have heard about her, knew her as Attie Bostick. Therefore, I felt compelled to write *Called to China: Attie Bostick's Life and Missionary Letters from China: 1900 to 1943*, so that others could learn about Attie's lifelong ministry as a Southern Baptist missionary to the Chinese people whom she learned to love and cherish. The book contains excerpts of numerous letters. I have left them essentially as the authors wrote them, although I made some changes, such as adding missing words and spelling out ampersands, months, and words like "Xmas."

I owe a huge debt of thanks to Edith (Edie) Jeter, the archivist at the Southern Baptist International Mission Board (IMB), in Richmond, Virginia, who copied over 1,500 pages of the letters and diaries of G. P., Wade, and Attie. My friend Ann Thompson of Shelby, North Carolina, assisted in the transcription of the letters and provided much needed encouragement to embark on this project. Margaret Jay of the Broad River Genealogical Society, Shelby, North Carolina, urged me to write this book. Doris Austell lent me her Bostick scrapbook containing several pictures included in this book. Betty Jo Putnam Carpenter provided material on the early Bosticks and on the Cool Springs Baptist Church in Forest City, North Carolina. Gladys Lowe of The Genealogical Society of Old Tryon County, Forest City, North Carolina, gave me Attie's New Testament, and Elizabeth Crabtree Wells of the Samford University Library, Birmingham, Alabama, provided guidance and direction. Dr. Wayne Flynt, a retired history professor emeritus of Auburn University, read the initial draft of the book, encouraged me, and helped me locate the editor of this book, Dr. Keith E. Durso. My scientist friend from China, Dr. C. H. Tsao, was educated by missionaries from the United States in his Junior High School Ye-Ho (Harmony) in Shanghai, and in one year of college at Soo-Chow University, Soo-Chow, near Shanghai. His positive impressions of missionaries and his insights were very helpful.

This work would not have been possible without my mother, who carefully preserved all of the Bostick family letters, pictures, and material she had collected over the years, including the papers she was given by two of G. P. Bostick's daughters, Bertha and Adelaide Bostick. All of this material eventually led me to contact Edie Jeter at the IMB. Both Bertha and Adelaide wrote about the Bostick missionaries in unpublished works, and their accounts have been utilized to provide eye-witness accounts of some of the events described in the book.

Finally, I want to thank my husband, James Hall Adams, Jr., who supported me during this project and whose love of and knowledge of history have provided the context of the work of the Bosticks.

Prologue

by James H. Adams, Jr.

Christian missionaries working in China in the late nineteenth and early twentieth centuries faced rejection and even hostility from some Chinese people. This anger was largely because the Chinese considered these missionaries to be the cultural arm of Western imperialism.[1] Such hostility also grew out of the conflict between the missionaries' religion and the Confucian establishment and the Chinese gentry-elite.[2] Nevertheless, missionaries were able to win over many Chinese through their good will and the relief they offered during sickness and famine. Many Chinese people warmed to the well-meaning and benevolent missionaries, even if they did not accept Christianity.

The Portuguese first brought Christianity to China in 1514. Ten years later Alessandro Valiganao obtained permission for the Jesuits to establish a mission on Chinese soil.[3] Under the Ming emperor, Kangxi, the Jesuits gained considerable influence at Court, but a dispute arose with Rome over the Jesuits's willingness to compromise with the Chinese practice of ancestor worship. This conflict led to a papal bull in 1742 that forbade Christians from performing Chinese rites, and the Ming dynasty responded by banning Christian proselytizing in China.[4]

Until the early nineteenth century Christianity had made little progress in China. The first Protestant missionary to the country was Robert Morrison of the London Missionary Society. He reached the international trading port of Guangzhou in 1807, but only made his first convert seven years later. By the 1830s missionaries from several European and American mission societies were working in China. In 1847 the French insisted that the ban on Christianity be lifted.[5] By 1860 France had obtained edicts from the Chinese government that removed many of the restrictions put in place under the Ming dynasty. Missionaries were then able to move freely about the country and could rent or purchase sites for missions in the interior of the country. Under the "most-favored-nation" clause, the missionaries from the

---

[1] This was, at least in part, because the western powers used any attack on missionaries as an excuse to extort enormous concessions and financial reparations from the Chinese government. This tactic became so expensive that the Chinese government provided special protection for missionaries and other foreigners in China.
[2] John King Fairbank and Merle Goldman, *China: A New History* (Cambridge, MA: Harvard University Press, 1992), 222.
[3] Ibid., 135.
[4] J. A. G. Roberts, *A Concise History of China* (Cambridge, MA: Harvard University Press, 1999), 150-51.
[5] Fairbank and Goldman, *China*, 222.

other western powers enjoyed the same privileges as the French. The Confucian establishment, responding to the legalization of Christianity and the Taiping Rebellion,[6] then began to spread malicious rumors that Christian missionaries engaged in immoral practices when men and women worshiped together and that they abused children placed in Christian orphanages. Despite these obstacles, the missionaries were successful in converting many Chinese to Christianity. By 1889 there were 37,000 Protestant converts, and by 1914, there were 250,000.[7]

---

[6] The Taiping Rebellion (1851-1864) was lead by Hong Xiuquan, a self-styled Christian who claimed to be God's second son. The rebellion cost 20 to 30 million lives but failed to overthrow the Qing dynasty.
[7] Roberts, *A Concise History of China*, 196.

CALLED TO CHINA

**Attie Bostick's Life and Missionary Letters
From China: 1900-1943**

Jane Price Suttle and Samuel Evans Bostick, March 4, 1908

Chapter One

ATTIE T. BOSTICK'S FAMILY

Go ye therefore, and teach all nations, baptizing them in the name of the Father, and of the Son, and of the Holy Ghost: Teaching them to observe all things whatsoever I have commanded you: and, lo, I am with you always, even unto the end of the world. (Matt. 28:19-20)[1]

Attie Texas Bostick's Family

In June 1900 Attie Texas Bostick left the security of her family and friends in the small town of Shelby, North Carolina, and sailed for Shanghai, China, to become a Baptist missionary. As a single, twenty-four-year-old woman, Attie knew that her parents, especially her mother, were extremely anxious and worried about her, but Attie felt deeply her call to missionary work in China and was determined to do God's will. She would ultimately have one of the longest missionary careers in China—forty-four years, during which she lived through famines, illnesses, the Boxer Rebellion, Chinese civil wars, the Japanese invasion of China in 1937, and two years of detention in internment camps.

On September 16, 1875, Attie was born on an isolated farm in the rolling foothills of the Appalachian Mountains. The Bostick farm was located in an area known as Floyd's Creek, six miles south of Forest City, North Carolina. Attie's mother, Jane Price Suttle, at age fifteen, married twenty-year-old Samuel Evans Bostick on October 15, 1850, and their children began arriving one year later. Jane and Samuel had seventeen children, eleven of whom survived to adulthood.[2] Their fifth child, George Pleasant, known both as G. P. and as Pleasant, was the first Bostick child to hear the call for mission work in China. Later both Attie and her brother Wade would also respond to God's call to serve as missionaries in China.

Attie's deeply religious parents and her grandparents were early settlers of the Piedmont section of southwestern North Carolina and were active church members in Rutherford County. John Bostick, the father of Samuel, was an organizing member of Cool Springs Baptist Church, which was founded in 1848. The congregation met in his home until 1855, when members raised enough money to erect a building. John sold the land on which his church built the first church building in the town of Burnt Chimney, North Carolina,

---

[1] All scripture references come from the King James Version.
[2] See Appendix. Two children were stillborn.

"The old home where we were all born from which G.P. went to Wake Forest." Attie Bostick, c. 1921

which was later named Forest City.³ Attie's mother was a member of the Baxter family, which, by 1921, had produced thirty-five ordained ministers.⁴ Thus, Attie's parents were surrounded by deeply committed Baptists, and no one was surprised when, in 1888, thirteen-year-old Attie was baptized at Zoar Baptist Church in Shelby, North Carolina.⁵

Farm life during the Civil War and the period of Reconstruction was hard and demanding. On their farm the Bosticks produced all of their food, and they grew cotton as their cash crop. They even made their own clothes, including the boys' and men's suits and shoes.⁶ The long hours of farming meant that some of the children had to work full time in the fields, so many of them received limited educations. This unfortunate situation was true for the oldest daughter, Sarah Louisa (Lou), and for the second daughter, Cynthia Judith (Judie), who had frail health her entire life and was unsuited for the heavy farming work. Judie was put in charge of caring for the younger children, and Attie, the sixteenth child and the baby of the family, was her favorite.

---

³ "Our Heritage (1848-1991)," First Baptist Church, Forest City, North Carolina, unpublished.
⁴ Untitled newspaper clipping, October 1921.
⁵ Operation Baptist Biography Data Form for *Living* Person, in the League, Attie T. Bostick folder, Foreign Mission Board Correspondence Collection (FMBCC), Box 33, Southern Baptist Historical Library and Archives (SBHLA), Nashville, TN.
⁶ Bertha Bostick, "The Missionary Bosticks," unpublished, 1932, 1, in the Bostick, George Pleasant folder, Baptist History file, SBHLA.

Despite the hardships of farm life and the demands of supporting a large family, Jane and Samuel continued to serve God. In an unpublished article titled "The Missionary Bosticks," Bertha May Bostick, one of G. P. Bostick's daughters, noted that despite

Cynthia Judith (Judie) Bostick, c. 1891

> the humbleness and crowded conditions of the home, and in spite of the tremendous amount of work to be done by the mother, she still found time and room to take in and entertain preachers and missionaries whenever they were in the vicinity, even to doing their washing and ironing with her own hands. It was chiefly this contact with these religious influences that turned the minds and hearts of the three 'missionary Bosticks' into religious work.
>
> G. P. has been heard to say that the first missionary seeds were sown in his heart when they had had eight Baptist preachers, among them, Dr. Hartwell, a returned missionary from China, in their home as guests.[7]

The visits by the missionaries had a profound effect on G. P., Wade, and Attie, for each was determined "to fit themselves with an education for service in the kingdom; and it was with great sacrifice and long years of hard work that this education was gained by each of them—not only sacrifice on the part of members of the family, who were glad to make it possible for these members to enter into so high a calling, but also on the part of each of these three consecrated members themselves. Each of them, after finishing high school, taught for awhile, living plainly that they might save up enough to go to college."[8] To provide better educational opportunities for their younger children, sometime in the 1880s, when Attie was still a young girl, Samuel and Jane Bostick moved their family twenty-five miles east from their farm in Rutherford County to the small town of Shelby, North Carolina.

The visiting missionaries were not the only people who influenced Attie during her early years. Later in life, she remembered the influence of her older sister Judie, who loved her church, particularly its support of foreign missions, and who often talked about how wonderful it was to be called to missionary work.

---

[7] Ibid. Jesse B. Hartwell served in China from 1858-1912.
[8] Ibid.

The First Bostick Missionary

The first Bostick to travel to the China mission field was G. P. He was seventeen years older than Attie and had attended college during her early childhood. G. P. heard God's call to preach soon after he was baptized at Floyd's Creek Baptist Church in 1873. In 1878, after graduating from high school in Boiling Springs, North Carolina, he entered Wake Forest College, near Raleigh, North Carolina. He worked his way through college by operating an "eating house" for students. Being the business manager and buyer enabled G. P. to employ several students who were also working their way through college. Lena Bostick, G. P.'s third wife, characterized her husband's college years as being "a keen satisfaction to him to know that while he was making his own way he was also helping other boys to make theirs. That was a life long characteristic. Eyes to see and a heart to help."[9]

After graduating from college in 1882, G. P. was ordained as a minister in May 1882 at New Hope Baptist Church near Raleigh.[10] He then attended seminary at Southern Baptist Theological Seminary in Louisville, Kentucky, graduating in 1885. While pastoring a nearby country church in Brownsboro, Kentucky, G. P. met his future wife, Bertha Belle Bryan.[11] They were married on October 20, 1887, in Brownsboro.[12]

After their marriage, the couple moved to North Carolina in order to find a place to organize a church for Baptists without a church home. G. P. found such a place in Concord, which was located in the rolling hills of southwestern North Carolina, and approximately one hundred miles east of his boyhood home. There G. P. began the work of reaching out to both Baptists and the unchurched. Soon after organizing a Baptist church in Concord, G. P. was called to pastor the First Baptist Church in Durham, North Carolina. On August 31, 1888, the young couple's daughter, Adelaide Price, was born.[13]

God continued to work in G. P.'s life, this time calling him to China. He prepared his church in Durham for his departure by preaching a sermon on Psalm 9:17, "The wicked shall be turned into hell, with all the nations that forget God." He made a strong case "for missions as God's appointed way to

---

[9] Lena Stover Bostick, *An Ambassador for Christ: George Pleasant Bostick*, 2nd ed. (Luray, VA: self published, n.d.), 4. This booklet can be found in the Bostick, George Pleasant folder, Baptist History file, SBHLA.
[10] Ibid., 4.
[11] Operation Baptist Biography Data Form for *Deceased* Person, in the Bostick, George Pleasant folder, Baptist History file, SBHLA.
[12] A page torn from the Bostick family Bible in the author's possession.
[13] "Data on Family of G. P. Bostick," compiled by Adelaide P. Bostick, April 1966, unpublished, 1, in the Bostick, George Pleasant folder, Baptist History file, SBHLA.

"G. P. Bostick and first wife, Bertha Belle Bryan Bostick, taken while pastor at Durham, shortly after their marriage in 1887," -Adelaide Bostick

reach and save the lost throughout the whole world."[14] The church supported G. P.'s call to foreign mission work, and in early 1889 the Southern Baptist Foreign Mission Board (FMB) appointed him to serve in China. G. P. and his family sailed for China in May 1889.

G. P.'s response to God's call to become a missionary thrilled the Bostick family. Attie recalled that she gazed in awe at her brother as she imagined the Chinese people with whom he would work. The entire family "watched for a letter from him. There was no air mail in those days . . . and it took a long time for a letter to come from China. Sometimes I'd see my mother wiping away tears on her apron, as she worked. I'd snuggle up to her quietly and kiss her. I know she was thinking of Pleasant. He had a wife and a baby daughter and Mother worried about them, too." When G. P.'s first letter arrived, "It was a day of rejoicing when there was finally a letter with a Chinese stamp. We almost wore it out reading it, and passing it around. Judie slept with it under her pillow. Of course we all wrote to Pleasant, but it was always Judie who was the faithful letter-writer of the family."[15] The example of an elder brother serving in China inspired Attie, and she took great interest in his work and followed his advice faithfully.

Despite opening their home to pastors and missionaries, and despite their strong religious beliefs, Jane and Samuel Bostick found it difficult to accept that their son was serving God in so distant a land. Letting go of a child who was called to a place so distant and so different from the security and safety of family and the farm was almost too great for them to bear.

G. P.'s Tragedy

G. P. and Bertha initially went to Tungchow (now Tongzhou)[16], located twenty miles east of Peking (now Beijing), where they studied the Chinese language. Bertha became ill on May 3, 1890, while G. P. was attending a General Missionary Conference in Shanghai, 550 miles from home. A doctor diagnosed Bertha as having small pox. Notified of his wife's illness, G. P. tried desperately to get home to be with his wife, but he learned when he was twenty miles from home that his twenty-five-year-old wife had already died on May 8.

In a newspaper article he wrote for friends in Cleveland and Rutherford Counties, North Carolina, G. P. described Bertha as his "most constant and best earthly help." Though he grieved the loss of his beloved wife, he never lost

---
[14] Bostick, *An Ambassador for Christ*, 5.
[15] Quoted in Edith Limer Ledbetter, "The Finest Missionary of Us All," *Royal Service,* June 1960, 38.
[16] See appendix three for a complete list of place names mentioned in this book.

faith in God. Bertha's death, G. P. wrote,

> is a mysterious dealing of a kind, loving Father. I do not ask Him to explain to me, but only to give grace to aid me in waiting and working and believing in the midst of mystery. Already He has blessed me in giving comfort and trust for still more. . . . To all the dear Christian readers who will grieve with me, let me say that God is comforting and will comfort me and you in all such times, if we trust Him. May this early death of the one who some of you loved to support only stimulate us all to a more earnest zeal for Christ our Master. Our end, too, is not far away. May we all be ready.[17]

"Adelaide P. Bostick, age 2 years, 7 months. March 1891" –Adelaide Bostick. (Made in Eminence, KY after Adelaide's mother, Bertha died, and she lived with her maternal grandfather and aunts.)

Bertha's death also had a profound effect on other missionaries. The Annual of the Southern Baptist Convention for 1891 described the atmosphere among Baptist missionaries in China: "During the whole year this mission has been draped in mourning. . . Mrs. Bertha Bostick . . . was naturally gifted, highly educated, and eminently adorned with the graces of missionary spirit. She was not merely the wife of a missionary—she was a missionary herself in deed and in truth."[18]

Bertha's death left G. P. with the care of their twenty-month-old child, Adelaide. He decided to send his daughter to live with her maternal grandfather and aunts in Brownsboro, Kentucky. A woman missionary accompanied Adelaide from Shanghai to Chicago, where her grandfather, Dr. Stanton Pierce Bryan, met her and took her to his home. Adelaide grew up in the care of Dr. Bryan and his two unmarried daughters, Daisy and Lillian.[19] G. P. remained in China to continue his mission work.

---

[17] Untitled newspaper clipping, May 17, 1890.
[18] *Annual*, Southern Baptist Convention (SBC), 1891, xxi.
[19] Adelaide P. Bostick, *Recollections of Dr. Stanton Pierce Bryan, Brownsboro Physician 1854-1894* (Crestwood, KY: Oldham County Historical Society, 1962), 10.

G. P.'s Remarriage

The year 1890 was also when Southern Baptist missionaries in Tungchow wrote the "Articles of Agreement," in which they declared that their work would be exclusively evangelistic, and that they would receive no public or institutional funds for their salaries. Instead, they agreed to receive support from local churches in the United States in order to cover their expenses, including their purchases of tracts and books, and their travel. They opposed providing charity to the Chinese, serving as pastors or school teachers, and "meddling in Chinese lawsuits." Several Baptist missionaries from different mission stations signed the document, including T. P. and Martha Crawford; Lottie Moon; C. W. and Anna Pruitt; Thomas J. (T. J.) and Florence League; Fannie Knight; Laura Barton; G. P. Bostick; and Mary Thornton. Of these missionaries, only Moon and the Pruitts remained with the FMB; the others, however, did not. Despite losing some of its missionaries, the FMB wished them "Godspeed."[20] Leaving their Southern Baptist affiliation allowed them to dress and live as the Chinese, which enabled them to reduce their living expenses from $600 to $300 per year; however, it also meant that their living conditions would be even more difficult.[21]

Mary Jane Thornton, one of the signers of the "Articles of Agreement," had arrived in China on August 9, 1890, as a Southern Baptist missionary. Born in December 1862 in Tuscaloosa, Alabama, Mary's father was killed in the Civil War, leaving her mother to support two young children. Despite these difficulties, Mary attended college at Alabama Central College in Tuscaloosa, graduating in 1889. One of her close friends, Susie V. Sheppard, described her fellow classmate as being "tall, erect, with dark hair and hazel eyes, fine strong face often lighted with contagious humor, whom the writer soon came to know well enough to nickname, 'Lang.'"[22]

Sometime in the late winter or early spring of 1889, Mary spoke to the pastor of Tuscaloosa Baptist Church about her call to missions. She applied to the FMB and named China as her preferred mission field assignment. The FMB accepted Mary's application and appointed her to help the well-known Southern Baptist missionary Lottie Moon, at Pingtu.[23]

---

[20] *Annual*, SBC, 1891, xix.
[21] Susie V. Sheppard, "Sketch of One of the First Three Missionaries sent to China by the First 'Lottie Moon Christmas Offering,' 1888, Mary Thornton," unpublished manuscript (September 9, 1942), 3, in the Bostick Family Correspondence folder (Mary Thornton Bostick), FMBCC, Box 8, SBHLA.
[22] Ibid., 1.
[23] Ibid., 1-2.

"G. P. Bostick and Mary Thornton Bostick, soon after marriage 1892."-Adelaide Bostick

On June 15, 1890, a farewell service was held for Mary prior to her departure for China. The Reverend J. G. Thornton spoke on "Bible Rules for Christian Giving," and the hymn "No More Good Byes" ended the service.[24] With the love and support of her family, friends, and church, Mary sailed for China. Though she was scheduled to serve with Lottie Moon in Pingtu, Mary ended up working in Tungchow.[25]

In a letter to her friend Susie Sheppard, Mary described the primitive living conditions on the mission field. The houses had dirt floors, and the windows were covered by paper greased in order to allow light to penetrate. The beds were made of bricks that were hollow inside with a flue so that a fire could heat them in the winter. Covers were spread over the brick beds in an attempt to make them comfortable. Mary explained that the streets were barren and that dead "things," along with any kind of refuse, were thrown into them. Missionaries traveled by shantze carried by coolies. She described one trip during which she was accompanied by a female servant. The roads on which they traveled were covered with mud that was nearly up to the knees, and their shantze turned over several times. Another obstacle some women missionaries faced was that unmarried women were unable to travel with a man because it would be scandalous.[26]

Despite the harsh living conditions, Mary fell in love with G. P. Bostick while they were both serving in Tungchow, and they were married on October 25, 1891. They had two children: Bertha (1893) and Martha (1894), who was called Mattie.

---

[24] "Farewell Services of Bethel Church, to Sister Mary J. Thornton, Missionary to China. 10 A.M., June 15, 1890," in the Bostick Family Correspondence folder (Mary Thornton Bostick), FMBCC, Box 8, SBHLA.
[25] See *Annual*, SBC, 1891, xviii.
[26] Mary Thornton to Susie Sheppard, April 12, 1891, in the Bostick Family Correspondence folder (Mary Thornton Bostick), FMBCC, Box 8, SBHLA.

G. P. and Mary Bostick, (l) Martha (Mattie) and (r) Bertha, c. 1896

In 1896 G. P., Mary, and their two daughters returned to the United States on furlough. Stanton Bryan, who had been caring for G. P.'s eldest daughter, Adelaide, had died in 1894, so Adelaide joined her new family, which settled in Shelby, North Carolina. While on furlough, Mary gave birth to her third child, Samuel Crawford, on December 22, 1896.[27]

During his furlough, G. P. traveled throughout the countryside, speaking in churches about China's millions of lost souls. Whenever he spoke near the Bostick home in Shelby, family members would ride in carriages and buggies to hear him preach.

---

[27] The child was named after his paternal grandfather and the missionary Tarleton Perry (T. P.) Crawford (1821-1902).

Attie's Call and Preparation for Her Journey

In 1889, prior to going to China for the first time, G. P. preached a sermon on Mark 14:8: "She hath done what she could." In an interview given when she was eighty-four years old, Attie recalled the effect that sermon had on her: "That day God spoke to me, and said that I would not be doing all that I could unless I was willing to go to China, too. Judie was not there that day, and I could hardly wait to get home and tell her. I had been her pet from the time I was a baby, and I know she would rejoice with me. Of course she did!"[28] Thus, at the age of fourteen, Attie believed that God had called her to China, but she knew that she would have to get an education before joining her brother on the mission field.

G. P. always supported Attie in her quest for an education, serving as her guide and mentor. On June 17, 1891, he wrote his fifteen-year-old sister Attie from Tungchow, encouraging her to "improve her mind" and not to spend much time thinking about boys so that she would "become a very useful woman."[29]

Attie followed her older brother's advice and attended Jones Seminary, located in All Healing Springs, North Carolina.[30] In the late 1880s in rural North Carolina, farm children who wanted a high school education attended boarding schools known as academies or seminaries. Despite living in a time when few girls were educated, and despite growing up in a family in which most of the children did not attend school beyond the third grade, Attie was determined to complete high school and then earn a college degree.

Judson College

Following her graduation from Jones Seminary in June 1894, Attie taught for two years in country schools in Cleveland County, North Carolina, to earn money to attend college. In 1896 she entered Judson College, a Baptist college for women located in Marion, Alabama, and named for Ann Hasseltine Judson, the first wife of Adoniram Judson. Judson College was located a great distance from Attie's home in Shelby, North Carolina, which meant that she had to spend holidays in Marion rather than at home with her family. Attie perhaps chose Judson because the college

---

[28] Quoted in Ledbetter, "The Finest Missionary of Us All," 39-40. See also Attie's Application for Appointment as Missionary, Foreign Mission Board, Southern Baptist Convention, [3], in the League, Attie T. Bostick folder, FMBCC, Box 33, SBHLA.
[29] G. P. Bostick to Attie Bostick, June 17, 1891. G. P. Bostick's letters cited throughout this book can be found in the FMBCC, Box 8, SBHLA.
[30] Application for Appointment as Missionary, Foreign Mission Board, Southern Baptist Convention, [2].

supported missions through the Ann Hasseltine Missionary Society. Willie Kelly, from Marion, Alabama, was a Baptist missionary to China, and the Judson College students sent money to support her work.[31]

Few records remain from the period that Attie attended Judson. The college yearbook, the *Judson Conversationalist*, began publication in 1897, but did not include any pictures. In the 1898 edition of the yearbook, Attie wrote an article for the Missionary Society and the Prayer Meeting, in which she described the group's study of materials provided by the Woman's Missionary Society. In her article Attie lamented that "over three thousand [Chinese] die daily! Reader, are you aware of this awful fact, and do you know you are responsible for their souls? You and I and every one that has the light are responsible for those who die without it. We expect soon to send Miss Kelly $24, which is for the clothing and schooling of a little Chinese girl."[32]

While at Judson, Attie studied music, voice, and elocution.[33] In 1898 she also participated in the graduating class's production of Shakespeare's *As You Like It*, playing the role of Duke senior.[34] She was elected class secretary and read her essay, "God is in the Heaven and All is Well on the Earth," at the June 1, 1898, commencement exercises, during which she received her AB degree. In the class of twenty-five young women graduates, Attie was the only student not from Alabama.[35]

Following college, Attie taught in a textile mill school in Gastonia, North Carolina, for two years. She used this time to save money and to raise support to fulfill her call to the Chinese mission field. By this time she had decided to go to China as part of the Gospel Mission program, which T. P. Crawford had organized in 1894. Missionaries in this program believed in raising their own funds to support their mission work in China, attempted to live like the Chinese (including wearing Chinese clothes, eating Chinese food, and living in

---

[31] Wayne Flynt and Gerald W. Berkley, *Taking Christianity to China: Alabama Missionaries in the Middle Kingdom, 1850-1950* (Tuscaloosa: The University of Alabama Press, 1997), 21; Frances Drew Hamilton and Elizabeth Crabtree Wells, *Daughters of the Dream: Judson College 1838-1988* (Marion, AL: Judson College, 1989), 81.
[32] *Judson Conversationalist* (Birmingham, AL: Rogers, Printer, 1898), 2:27.
[33] Judson Institute Catalogue, Marion, AL, 1897-98 (Montgomery, AL: Alabama Printing Company, 1898), 10, 12, 14.
[34] Ibid, 60.
[35] Ibid, 62.

Missionaries in Taian, Shantung Province, c. 1892
Back row: Mary Thornton Bostick, D. W. Herring; T. J. League
Second row: G. P. Bostick, T. P. Crawford, Martha Crawford, Mr. King
Front row: ___, ___, Florence League

Chinese-styled homes), and were independent of the Southern Baptist FMB.[36] Thus, as Attie prepared to go to China, she enlisted financial support from the First Baptist Church in Gastonia, where she was an active member. Attie's sister Judie also financially contributed to Attie's work throughout her life.

The Bosticks' Return to China

After G. P.'s family returned to China in the summer of 1898, Mary wrote her mother-in-law, Jane Bostick, describing the children's good behavior on their voyage to China on the steamer, life in China, and recurrent problems with thieves. At the time she wrote this letter, Mary was pregnant with her fourth child, George Thornton, who was born later that year on December 24. At the end of the letter, Mary related that she and G. P. were eager to know of Attie's plans about coming to China. She advised that it would be best if Attie found a "good man and either marry before she comes or within a year or two afterwards. I believe a married woman can [do] more good here than a single one and then it is so hard on an unmarried man or woman here."[37]

---

[36] W. B. Glass, "Gospel Mission Movement (North and Central China)," in *Encyclopedia of Southern Baptists* (Nashville: Broadman Press, 1958), 1:571; Catherine B. Allen, *The New Lottie Moon Story* (Nashville: Broadman Press, 1980), 196.
[37] Mary Thornton Bostick to Jane Bostick, July 13, 1898, in FMBCC, Box 8, SBHLA.

Whether married or single, however, women were essential to the success of the gospel in China. As Wayne Flynt and Gerald W. Berkley observed: "Without the presence of women no substantial Protestant missionary effort would have occurred in China. . . . Officially, Chinese women were discouraged from traveling about in public, conversing with males, attending school, or receiving intimate examinations by a male physician. If Chinese women were to be saved, Western women would have to do the evangelizing."[38] Flynt and Berkley also debunked the myth that women needed to be married in order to be successful missionaries. Because married women were often "too busy to evangelize because they were tending families or falling victim to illnesses associated with childbirth and child rearing," the "successful evangelizing of Chinese women . . . depended heavily on single female missionaries."[39]

G. P. eagerly anticipated the time when Attie could join the Gospel Mission work in Taian (now Tai'an), Shantung (now Shandong) Province. Missionaries stationed there included G. P. and Mary Bostick, D. W. Herring; Mr. King; T. P. and Martha Crawford; Mr. Blalock; Fanny Knight; and T. J. and Florence League. In his letter of May 3, 1898, G. P. provided Attie with detailed instructions on when to travel and exactly what to bring. He told his sister to bring a wood stove, dresses for Adelaide, thread to make stockings, knitting yarn, and knitting needles.[40]

While G. P. prepared his sister for her journey, he also prepared his parents to let Attie go. The Bosticks were extremely anxious about her desire to serve as a missionary, having lost their daughter-in-law Bertha to small pox within a year of her arrival in China. Given their reluctance to allow their youngest child to embark on such a dangerous mission, G. P. tried to reassure his parents about Attie's safety: "My dear father, . . . I do most earnestly pray that God may give you one and all the needed grace for the separation in Attie's leaving and that he may enable you and mother to realize how highly honored you are in having him call so many of your children into this the greatest of all work and the one nearest to his own heart."[41]

In 1900 Jane and Samuel Bostick said good-bye to another child leaving for China. After six years of studying to receive a high school and college education, teaching, living frugally, saving money, and raising financial support, Attie, unmarried yet faithful to her call, was finally ready to sail to the land of her dreams—China.

---

[38] Flynt and Berkley, *Taking Christianity to China*, 191.
[39] Ibid., 192.
[40] G. P. Bostick to Attie Bostick, May 3, 1899.
[41] G. P. Bostick to Samuel Bostick, July 4, 1899.

Attie Texas Bostick, Shelby, NC, c.1900

Chapter Two

ATTIE'S YEARS WITH THE GOSPEL MISSION PROGRAM
1900-1915

How beautiful upon the mountains are the feet of him that bringeth good tidings, that publisheth peace; that bringeth good tidings of good, that publisheth salvation; that saith unto Zion, Thy God reigneth! (Isa. 52:7)

Attie's Arrival in China

Attie arrived in Shanghai, China, in June 1900 at the height of the Boxer Rebellion. Anti-foreign sentiment had been rising for a number of years in China, and the rebellion had its origins in the popular resentment of the foreign domination of China. The Boxer Rebellion began in Shantung Province in a densely populated and impoverished area along the Yellow River. The importation of machine-spun yard had depressed the value of cotton grown in that area, increasing the poverty of the Chinese farmers.[1]

Determined Catholic missionaries had been operating in Shantung Province for many years, and they attracted converts partly by supporting them in lawsuits against non-Christians.[2] This practice heightened the resentment toward all missionaries, who were seen as extensions of the foreign domination of China.

The Chinese people, having suffered from famines and recent floods, were also experiencing a drought in 1900.[3] The social and economic stress caused by these natural disasters found an outlet in the Spirit Boxer Movement, which combined martial arts with the belief in spirit possession. The Boxers, after performing rituals and getting into a trance-like state, were ready to do battle, confident that they would be protected from being harmed by swords and bullets.[4] Their objective was to support the Qing dynasty and destroy the foreigners in their country.

The Boxer Rebellion spread rapidly across northern China, gaining the support of Manchu princes and even the Empress Dowager, who formally declared war on all foreign powers occupying China.[5] In northern China, the governor of Shansi (now Shanxi) Province, Yu Xian, captured and "executed forty-four men, women, and children from missionary families."[6] Adelaide Bostick, the eldest daughter of G. P. Bostick, wrote that in 1900, when she was age twelve, her family and other

---

[1] J. A. G. Roberts, *A Concise History of China* (Cambridge, MA: Harvard University Press, 1999), 201.
[2] Ibid.; John King Fairbank and Merle Goldman, *China: A New History* (Cambridge, MA: Harvard University Press, 1992), 230.
[3] Roberts, *A Concise History*, 201.
[4] Fairbank and Goldman, *China*, 230.
[5] Ibid., 231. These foreign powers included England, France, Germany, Portugal, and the United States.
[6] Roberts, *A Concise History of China*, 202.

missionary families had to flee to the coast to escape the violence resulting from the rebellion.[7]

During the summer of 1900, 250 foreigners (mostly missionaries) and thousands of Chinese Christians were slaughtered. Also, about 1,000 foreign citizens and foreign troops, along with 3,000 Chinese Christians, were trapped in the Peking legation quarter for a month and a half. The siege was finally lifted when foreign troops liberated the city. Military expeditions under the supervision of the German field marshal Alfred Graf von Waldersee were then sent out to towns supporting Boxer activity, suppressing the rebellion.[8]

After the rebellion was crushed, the foreign powers in China then demanded and received official apologies from Chinese government officials. Foreign governments also called for the execution of officers who supported the rebellion, the destruction of twenty-five Qing forts, and a payment of $333 million, plus interest, over forty years. With interest, this payment amounted to more than $600 million.[9] The United States waived its part of the reparation payments, but used payments extracted from the Chinese government for "damages" caused by the rebellion to establish Qinghua University in Peking.[10]

Attie arrived in China during the turbulent summer of 1900. She stayed with the Southern Baptist missionary Willie Kelly, who was living in the port city of Shanghai, which was not directly affected by the Boxer Rebellion. There Attie learned the language and lived in safety from June 1900 until September 1901.

Attie's Description of Her Early Days in China

Attie's departure from her family, despite her deep sense of call, was nonetheless painful and difficult. She doubted that she could ever leave home again with the same sense of composure as she had in the spring of 1900. In her letter of December 7, 1900, Attie described her trip to her sister Judie. The journey to China had been long and physically demanding. With all of her worldly goods packed into a steamer trunk, Attie boarded a train in Shelby, North Carolina, and traveled first to Asheville, North Carolina. She wrote that the stress of the trip had affected her physically. She lost sleep and caught a cold in Asheville, then her face broke out and a sty appeared on her left eye. The sea voyage, however, revived her spirits and her appetite.[11]

---

[7] "Data on Family of G. P. Bostick," compiled by Adelaide P. Bostick, April 1966, unpublished, 1, in the Bostick, George Pleasant folder, Baptist History file, Southern Baptist Historical Library and Archives (SBHLA), Nashville, TN.
[8] Roberts, *A Concise History of China*, 202.
[9] Fairbank and Goldman, *China*, 232.
[10] Roberts, *A Concise History of China*, 202.
[11] Attie Bostick to Judie Bostick, December 7, 1900. All of Attie Bostick's letters cited throughout this book can be found in the Foreign Mission Board Correspondence Collection (FMBCC), Box 33, Southern Baptist Historical Library and Archives (SBHLA), Nashville, TN. Attie's letters are filed under her married name, League.

In writing to Judie, Attie also sought to reassure her sister, who apparently considered her life a failure because she was not able to do the things that her favorite sister, Attie, could do. Attie tried to encourage her, stating:

> I often think of you, in doing the work you do, and I know your health and circumstances often tend to make you gloomy and cause you to feel that your life is no avail, but you know it is the "faithful one" who is promised the crown of life and faithful doesn't always mean successful either. Yes, I think we are all inclined to have the blues sometimes and I often think a good, healthy cry does us good, but I don't believe we ought to give way to these feelings too much.[12]

Unlike her sister, however, Attie, felt fulfilled in her work: "I am very happy and God has been very good to me during all this waiting and I feel that He has taught me lessons which I otherwise could not have learned. I am not deprived of any of the necessities of life either. Does mother believe this? Well, it is true and I haven't eaten any millet yet and have had as nice onions as I could get out of her kitchen."[13]

With Christmas approaching, Attie knew that Judie would want to do something to make her happy, but she encouraged her sister to "make those about you happy. Don't think of me and wish you could send me something for I am happy and I know if you had the opportunity you would give me something and so I appreciate that just the same."[14]

Attie also mentioned the kindness that the missionaries T. J. and Florence League had shown her on the passage to China and after they arrived in the country: "We were joking today about my appetite and Mrs. League was teasing me about writing her that I would not need a lunch basket and then eating like I did. Mr. League said I looked as if I had started to go to my own funeral." ✶ Attie noted that her poor physical appearance had made her appear "frightful. But I soon revived and my sea voyage gave me such an appetite that I haven't lost it yet, and I believe it did my whole system good."[15]

Part of the year, Attie confided to Judie, "seems like a dream to me and I often wonder if I won't some day awake and find I am dreaming that I am in China. I know I could never leave home again under the same circumstances with the same composure that I left with in the spring but I thank God that He gave me strength to stand it all as well as I did. He has promised us all the strength if we will but look to Him for it."[16]

---

[12] Ibid. ✶ Later Attie married Mr. League (p. 133)
[13] Ibid.
[14] Ibid.
[15] Ibid.
[16] Ibid.

In another letter to Judie, dated February 15, 1901, Attie noted that the Chinese New Year was approaching and that the Chinese were "preparing for it as much or more than we prepare for Christmas. Those who live near us, we see cleaning chickens, cleaning up their houses and such like, all the time. They expect a big time."[17]

In a letter to Attie, Judie had informed her sister that their parents were thinking of selling the "home place," the family's farm at Floyd's Creek in Rutherford County, North Carolina. The thought of her parents selling the farm where she grew up saddened Attie: "I would feel rather sad to think of leaving the place which has been our home for so long. I am afraid Mother would never be satisfied up town, but she knows best what ought to suit her. I do think Pa and Mother have both done enough in their lifetime not to work hard in their old age, but live on what they already have. They have had a hard time most all their lives, but God has blessed them in it."[18]

After the suppression of the Boxer Rebellion, conditions in China had become safe enough by the fall of 1901 for missionaries to return to the interior of China. In September 1901 Attie moved to Taian (now Tai'an), Shantung (now Shandong) Province, where she joined other members of the Gospel Mission. In an undated photograph of missionaries in Taian, the following are pictured: G. P. and Mary Thornton Bostick; D. W. Herring; Mr. King; T. P. and Martha Crawford; Miss Fanny Knight; and T. J. and Florence League. Southern Baptists also had missionaries in the province, but none in Taian.

---

[17] Attie Bostick to Judie Bostick, February 15, 1901.
[18] Ibid.

Gospel Mission Group at Taian, c. 1901
Back row: G. P. Bostick, ___, ___, David W. Herring, ___.
Second row: Mary T. Bostick, T. P. Crawford, Martha Crawford, W.D. King
Front row: Fanny Knight, Florence League, T. J. League

Another Tragedy for G. P.

G. P. Bostick initially worked in Taian, but he felt called to go farther into the interior. When he informed "the local official at Taian . . . of his purpose to move to Pochow [now Bozhou, Anhui Province] the official said, 'I beg you, Mr. Bostick, not to go to a place like that, and take your children. They are wild men and will kill you before breakfast.'"[19]

Despite being warned about going to Pochow, G. P. began work there on a new mission station in early 1903. His first task was to build a large home to accommodate his wife and five children and the other missionary families who would be living in Pochow, a city of approximately 150,000 people that was located in an isolated area approximately thirty-five miles from the nearest train station. Travel, much of which was done by wheelbarrow over the muddy dirt roads, was tedious and difficult. No other foreign missionaries had ever been to Pochow, but G. P. was excited about the location and the people to whom he and his co-workers would present the gospel.

---

[19] Lena Stover Bostick, *An Ambassador for Christ: George Pleasant Bostick*, 2nd ed. (Luray, VA: self published, n.d.), 8, in the Bostick, George Pleasant folder, Baptist History file, SBHLA.

Wade and Flora Bostick, Pochow, Anhwei Province, c. 1906

G. P. was also anticipating the arrival of his brother and sister-in-law, Wade and Flora Bostick, who were planning to serve with him in Pochow. A year older than Attie, Wade too had felt called to China, and he eventually became the third Bostick to travel to the China mission field. Following in G. P.'s footsteps, Wade worked his way through college at Wake Forest, where he met Flora Holloway, a student at Meredith College in Raleigh, North Carolina. They were married on October 23, 1901, in Raleigh. After graduating from college with a BA degree, Wade served several country churches in preparation for the mission field.[20]

While G. P. was building his home in Pochow, Mary and the children were living in Chefoo (now Yantai), the coastal city to which the family had fled in 1900 during the Boxer Rebellion. In March 1903 Mary contracted pneumonia and died on March 25 at the age of forty-one. The Bostick's daughter Bertha, who had just turned ten on March 9, 1903, later described her mother as spending most "of her time . . . being a wife and mother, but her heart was in the mission work, along with her husband; and she longed for the time when she could be free to go out among the Chinese women, at forty years of age (for that was the custom among Chinese women, to remain quietly at home raising their children, until they were considered free to go out, at the age of forty) to carry the gospel message to the women." But that was not to be. G. P. had the following inscription engraved on Mary's tombstone: "She hath done what she could, and is at rest with Jesus."[21]

By September 1904 G. P. had completed the building of the home/mission station in Pochow. Because most Chinese houses were "little more than mud huts," and because lumber was scarce, he had built "a nine room, two story brick house, . . . to accommodate two or three mission families, with a chapel in

---

[20] Operation Baptist Biography Data Form for *Deceased* Person, FMBCC, Box 8, SBHLA.
[21] Bostick, Mary Jane (Thornton) folder, Baptist History file, SBHLA.

G. P. Bostick with Chinese students, Pochow, Anhwei Province, c.1922

Brick house designed and constructed by G. P. Bostick in 1904

the edge of the yard."[22] Attie and G. P.'s five children (Adelaide, Bertha, Mattie, Sam, and Thornton) soon joined G. P. in their new home. Years later Attie described the hectic household. In addition to G. P. and his family, Wade and Flora Bostick arrived, having raised their own financial support through the Gospel Mission program. That winter, Mr. and Mrs. Blalock, two members of the Gospel Mission, also joined the Bosticks in Pochow. Thus, eleven people were living in the house, and Attie described herself as "the housekeeper!"[23] Attie also helped care for Flora when her children were born—Wade H., who was born on August 11, 1907 and Oreon, who was born on February 23, 1911.

The Ministry in Pochow

The numerous opportunities to preach the gospel offset any problems caused by the crowded conditions at the Bostick home. Bertha, who was eleven when she moved to Pochow, later recalled the activity at her home, which also served as a mission. At the chapel, "men callers were entertained . . . [and] preaching services were held for a number of years until there were enough Christians to build a church. The women were received in what was called the 'Guest Room'—a room downstairs which did not open into the other part of the house, but only on the veranda." The six adults "were the only missionaries

---

[22] Bertha Bostick, "The Missionary Bosticks," unpublished, 1932, 3, in the Bostick, George Pleasant folder, Baptist History file, SBHLA.
[23] Attie Bostick to Charles Maddry, November 28, 1936.

within a radius of sixty miles, or of two days travel, as travel went then, and within a radius of several million souls, who had never heard of the gospel."[24]

Despite the limitless opportunities to preach, Bertha recalled that the missionaries also encountered numerous "obstacles of ignorance, superstition, and prejudice." For example, before she, her siblings, and her Aunt Attie arrived in the city, "no white woman or child had ever been seen." The appearance of the first white women and children in the city caused quite a scene, and crowds followed them for months, even though the Americans wore Chinese clothes. At first, the Chinese feared them and called them "foreign devils." Eventually, however, the people began to trust the missionaries and sought them

> for help in sickness and accidents and troubles; for it was found that the missionaries had healing medicines, and could often bind and heal broken and cut limbs. . . . Although there was no doctor among the missionaries, they had simple home remedies always on hand; and they were often called on in the middle of the night for antidotes for poison by relatives of some person who had tried to commit suicide. One of the Bosticks remarked that in their first year there, they saved over a hundred attempted suicides from death.[25]

The missionaries took every opportunity to preach to visitors to the mission, which kept them so busy that they often went all day without eating. When not talking with Chinese seekers at the mission, the men journeyed throughout the area, traveling by bicycles, wheelbarrows, carts, or donkeys, and they often walked "from ten to twenty miles a day, stopping on the roadside, in market places, or on the streets of the cities, wherever a crowd congregated, to tell why they had left their own homes and people and land to come to their land, and to tell the gospel story." The women also traveled, going "out in wheelbarrows to the surrounding villages, visiting in some home where the women would crowd in, and sometimes talking to them, and answering questions until midnight."[26]

---

[24] Bostick, "The Missionary Bosticks," 3.
[25] Ibid.
[26] Ibid.

Back Row: Sam, Adelaide, Bertha, Mattie Bostick
Front row: Attie, G. P., Lena, Thornton Bostick, c. 1908

Attie's and G. P.'s Furloughs

In the spring of 1907, after serving in Pochow for three years, Attie, along with G. P. and his five children, returned to the United States on furlough. Unfortunately, no records exist concerning Attie's furlough. Records of G. P.'s furlough do exist and demonstrate that he had a rewarding one. He and his family lived in Nashville, Tennessee, where he enrolled the children in school and where he served as a "missionary-on-furlough."[27] While there, G. P. met Lena Stover and quickly proposed to her. Lena later described the event in her booklet, *An Ambassador for Christ: George Pleasant Bostick*:

G. P. Bostick and wife Lena Stover Bostick, c. 1907

> I was invited, rather urgently, to join the family in Nashville as his wife, and I can still say I am glad I accepted that loving and cordial invitation, although it meant that Attie would surrender her place to me and in due time return to her work in China.
>
> It was not an altogether easy assignment, becoming a little step-mama so suddenly. But balancing the love and character of the man who gave the invitation against any questions I might have had, made it not only possible but even attractive and desirable. And it proved to be the best choice I ever made.[28]

---

[27] Bostick, *An Ambassador for Christ*, 8.
[28] Ibid, 8-9.

Lena and G. P. Bostick, c. 1913

"My dog and me. For Thornton."— G. P. Bostick, c. 1913

In 1909 Lena developed cancer, which required major surgery and a two-year recovery period.[29] During this time she remained in Nashville and helped care for the children. G. P. returned to China in 1910 briefly, before returning to the United States. Two years later, Lena was cancer free and able to travel with G. P. to China and to join him in serving in Pochow. G. P. made the painful decision to have his children remain in the States so that they could continue their education.

Petitions for Southern Baptist Support

In 1909 Wade and Flora, who had remained in China, applied to the Southern Baptist Foreign Mission Board (FMB) to serve as Southern Baptist missionaries. During that year both Wade and G. P. petitioned the FMB to take over the support of the Pochow station.[30] Wade described the strategic location of the city, noting that it was

> by far the largest city [in the area] and is an important point, being the head of navigation on this river and is a big distribution center. . . . There is

---

[29] G. P. Bostick to R. J. Willingham, December 20, 1909. Robert Josiah (R. J.) Willingham was the corresponding secretary of the Foreign Mission Board from 1893 to 1914.
[30] G. P. Bostick to R. J. Willingham, December 30, 1909; and Wade Bostick to R. J. Willingham, November 8, 1909. Wade Bostick's letters can be found in the FMBCC, Box 8, SBHLA.

now in this field which is distinctively considered ours, five large cities with tens or maybe hundreds of market towns with a population of from a few hundred to 20 or 30 thousands of villages. In two of these cities, besides Pochow, we have baptized members. One of these places, Lu I, has been one of our best points and they have a house and lot there, in a good part of the city and well adapted to their use and it has been largely paid for by the natives.[31]

Wade's petitions proved to be fruitful. On November 18, 1909, Annie Jenkins Sallie, secretary for the Interior China Baptist Mission, made the following recommendation to the FMB: "Moved that we recommend the Board: 1st., to take on the Pochow and out-station work as per Bro. Bostick's request; 2nd., to appoint Mr. and Mrs. Wade Bostick as missionaries; 3rd., to seize upon the opportunities opened in this new field and send our workers immediately to man it; 4th., to take over the property at Tsi-ning-chow with a view to sending our new missionaries to man the field as soon as possible."[32] Southern Baptists approved the recommendation, and on May 4, 1910, they appointed Wade and Flora as Southern Baptist missionaries in Pochow.[33]

The FMB's 1911 report to the Southern Baptist Convention described Pochow as "the center of a large unworked territory. The field, for the evangelism of which we have become responsible, is about one hundred and thirty miles square in a densely populated section of the Great Plain, and covers six or eight counties in which no other Mission or any denomination is at present, working. Our Board has taken over this field, because the Gospel Mission brethren were unable to man it."[34] The report appealed for further support for this area, noting that approximately forty church members lived in Pochow, and four at the outstations. Chinese Christians were also preaching in the area and selling about 100 copies of scripture a day.[35]

Attie's Correspondence with the Foreign Mission Board

Following her yearlong furlough, Attie returned in 1908 to her mission work in Pochow, where she joined Wade and Flora, and Mr. and Mrs. Blalock. Also that year, Attie, although still affiliated with the Gospel Mission organization, began communicating with Robert J. Willingham, corresponding secretary of the Southern Baptist FMB. In her letter of November 25, Attie thanked Willingham for send-

---

[31] Wade Bostick to R. J. Willingham, November 8, 1909.
[32] Motion to FMB, November 18, 1909, in the Bostick, Wade D. folder, FMBCC, Box 8, SBHLA.
[33] Bostick, Wade D. folder, FMBCC, Box 8, SBHLA; *Annual*, Southern Baptist Convention (SBC), 1911, 215.
[34] *Annual*, SBC, 1911, 216.
[35] Ibid, 215.

ing her copies of the *Foreign Mission Journal,* and she also suggested that Southern Baptist missionaries could save $50 on their passages to and from China by traveling "second cabin." On a recent passage she had spoken with a Southern Baptist missionary who did not even know about the second cabin accommodations. As a result of this conversation, Attie stated what to her was obvious: "In view of the sacrifices so many people in the U.S. make to contribute to missions, do you not think it but just to them that the young men missionaries, at least should come Second Cabin and so save that fifty dollars?" To bolster her argument, Attie emphasized that she had "crossed three times on the cheap ticket and I think I fared better than most of the ones who were giving of their means to support me, and I believe most of your missionaries would gladly accept this passage if you would put it to them in this light." She apologized to Willingham "for offering this advice, unasked, but I am here where I feel very sorely the need of more laborers and in this way some means can be saved."[36]

In January 1912 Attie moved from Pochow back to Taian to help Mrs. Blalock, who had developed tuberculosis. She and her husband had decided to move farther north to the mountainous regions of Taian because of her illness.[37] Sometime during the year on a lengthy visit to Pochow, Attie apparently did some work in the city for the FMB. She mentioned to G. P., who had returned to work for the FMB in 1912, that she ought to be paid for her efforts. G. P. then communicated her request to the FMB's corresponding secretary. In a letter to Willingham in March 1913, Attie thanked him for his

> kind offer to give me three months salary for the time I have spent at Pochow, and it was at my own suggestion that anything was said about paying me anything in the first place. Still, after more deliberate and prayerful consideration of the matter, I do not feel able to accept anything. I had to make the trip anyway to move my things away and I should have wanted a visit of a month or two anyway. . . . It was a joy to do whatever I could among the girls and women with whom I had labored away for seven years and whom I love most tenderly and it goes without saying that my association with my own dear brother and his wife [Wade and Flora] was a pleasure and between the two brothers my trip there and back cost me practically nothing, so I felt more than repaid for the three months and more that I was away from Taian. But I thank you most kindly for the generous consideration you were making of my services there. I hope and pray the Board may soon be out of debt and that God may send forth more laborers, several to Pochow where four or five families more of earnest laborers would not be an over supply.[38]

---

[36] Attie Bostick to R. J. Willingham, November 25, 1908.
[37] Bostick, "The Missionary Bosticks," 3.
[38] Attie Bostick to R. J. Willingham, March 31, 1913.

The FMB's debt Attie mentioned was nearly $70,000 in 1913.

In between her two letters to Willingham, Attie continued to fulfill her ministry, often under difficult circumstances. The 1911 Southern Baptist *Annual* noted that "While Miss Attie Bostick is still being supported by Gospel Mission churches, we rejoice that she continues her faithful work at" [Pochow].[39] Along with Flora, Attie visited women in their homes, sharing the gospel with them and teaching them how to read the Bible. One girl whom Attie taught memorized over 400 verses of scripture in one year.[40]

The difficulties of doing mission work in China became even more challenging in 1911 when the country suffered a severe famine.[41] Wade described the dire situation in a letter to the Baptist newspaper in North Carolina, the *Biblical Recorder*. He lamented that "there is simply a multitude of faces around my front gate pleading for something to eat." Those faces haunted him, particularly when he prayed: "I never bow my head to say grace or raise my heart in prayer that my mind's eye does not go to the multitude of needy and my sympathy is so touched for them that I feel now that I will give to the very bottom of my pocketbook if there is not a great deal of giving from the outside. I often pray that the hearts of many people will be touched and that liberal giving will be the result." He also highlighted the magnitude of the disaster and the cost in human lives it could claim: "It is estimated that 3,000,000 people are in great need in this famine-stricken district, and that at least 1,000,000 will likely perish before the wheat is garnered if they do not receive help."[42] Wade's letter was later published in the *Charlotte Observer* and then read at a Ladies' Missionary Meeting of the First Baptist Church in Charlotte, North Carolina, and a sizeable collection was taken to aid the relief effort.

The famine also deeply affected Attie. Lottie Moon, in a letter to her nephew Luther Andrews, mentioned that Attie had written her, asking that "'for the sake of God and humanity, send all the help you can.'" Moon praised Attie, Wade, and Flora for "standing nobly amid all the awful horrors that rend their hearts daily."[43]

---

[39] *Annual*, SBC, 1911, 215.
[40] Ibid., 216.
[41] Severe flooding on the Yangtze River to the south of Pochow in the spring of 1911 could have contributed to this famine. The mounting discontent caused by the famine and the failures of the Qing dynasty led to its collapse in the fall of 1911.
[42] Wade Bostick, "The Famine in China," *Charlotte Observer*, undated newspaper clipping.
[43] Lottie Moon to William Luther Andrews, March 24, 1911, in *Send the Light: Lottie Moon's Letters and Other Writings*, ed. Keith Harper (Macon, GA: Mercer University Press, 2002), 437.

Mission Group in Chefoo, c. 1916
Back row center: Attie Bostick
Third row, 3rd from left: Lena Bostick
Second row, 2nd from left: G.P. Bostick

During the first fifteen years that Attie served in China, she was affiliated with the Gospel Mission program, with financial support coming either from the members of the congregation of First Baptist Church in Gastonia, North Carolina (1900-1907), or from other supporters. Attie served the Gospel Mission program and its supporters faithfully and courageously, despite the obstacles of living in a foreign land, being called a foreign devil, mourning the loss of a sister-in-law, living in crowded conditions, caring for several young children, and surviving a deadly famine. Added to these trials in China, she grieved over the death of her father, who died on January 11, 1910. In 1915 serious problems developed with some of the Gospel Mission missionaries, forcing Attie to reevaluate her relationship with that organization.

Chapter Three

ATTIE'S FIRST YEARS AS A SOUTHERN BAPTIST MISSIONARY
1916-1921

For thou art my rock and my fortress; therefore for thy name's sake lead me, and guide me. (Ps. 31:3)

Attie's Dilemma

In her letter of December 21, 1915, Attie apologized to her sister Judie for not writing more often, but she had been *"so* busy this autumn" that she found little time to write. She had also become disillusioned with the Gospel Mission program, particularly with some of the newer missionaries. "I haven't known what I ought to do," Attie confided to Judie, "and had to take one step at a time and even yet I cannot see it would be the wisest thing for me to apply to the [Southern Baptist Foreign Mission] Board just now. These other people still claim to be G. M. [Gospel Mission]. . . . They are *not* G. M., and their influence here is really hurtful . . ., so on their account and for the sake of the many years of Baptist work here, I feel I must go slowly and prayerfully."[1] Unfortunately, Attie did not elaborate on the problems caused by the divisive missionaries, though in a later letter to the corresponding secretary of the Southern Baptist Foreign Mission Board (FMB), she would provide more details.

Attie's life in China was not, however, completely consumed by her concerns about the Gospel Mission personnel. On January 6, 1916, she wrote two of her nieces, Adelaide and Bertha, thanking them for their Christmas gifts and describing her work with the Chinese and her Christmas celebration with her brother Wade and his family. In a paragraph that sounded like an apology, Attie informed Adelaide that she tried not to exasperate her friends and family by constantly apologizing for not writing more often:

> If I were much of a hand to apologize, I'd feel I must make many to you for not having written you *directly* since getting that pretty dress, but I go on the policy of *trying* to do my best and then not wear my friends out apologizing, and I believe you understand me well enough to have no desire for apologies. The dress came December 5th or 6th, and I was out in the village working from then till a week before Christmas when I stopped to get ready for Uncle Wade's family. The dress is a fine fit, and I like it very much. I

---
[1] Attie Bostick to Judie Bostick, December 21, 1915.

wore it to Mrs. Dawes' tea, with Flora a week ago yesterday p.m., and Mrs. Dawes, who is a very stylish woman, had many compliments both for it and my cravat. It will come in so nicely when I go to Peking in March to nurse Mattie [Attie's pregnant niece], and I thank you again and again for it.²

At Christmas Attie had the joy of hosting her brother Wade's family. Her nephew Wade "very much enjoyed playing with the other children of this community" and "cried when they left." Attie also noted that she had given her niece Oreon a doll.³

In her letter to Adelaide, Attie wrote that the missionary work in villages continued to go well, although she had been hampered by a "bad . . . cold, and the weather has been too cold, too. . . . The Chinese New Year comes February 3rd this year and there can't be much real earnest work done by visiting that month, as it is the only time of the year they have any holiday much. We have planned a two week meeting the last of the moon, and I hope we can get some good class work done."⁴

Adelaide's father, G. P. Bostick, wanted Attie to return home on furlough in 1916, but the thought of leaving China, even briefly, troubled her: "I can't get the consent of my mind to leave, with no one to go on with the work I am trying to do. And I haven't the money either. I received $290.37 last year and $160.00 more as passage money, but I had to use part of the latter for living expenses. I will have to use more for my other is 'clean out.'"⁵

In a letter to her niece Bertha, whom she affectionately called Berfy, Attie responded to Bertha's letter of November 21, "in which you wanted me to listen and see if I could hear you wishing me a Merry Christmas, [and which] must have gotten on a slow steamer for it didn't reach me till Thursday after Christmas."⁶ She also thanked Bertha for sending a copy of Fanny Crosby's autobiography, which arrived on Christmas night.

Attie also expressed her desire to hear about Adelaide's and Bertha's visit with T. J. and Florence League, who were on furlough: "I can hardly wait to hear from [you about] your visit to Mrs. League's for somehow I feel you all

---

² Attie Bostick to Adelaide Bostick, January 6, 1916. Mrs. Dawes was Laura Dawes, a Southern Baptist missionary from 1910 to 1932. Mattie was G. P. and Mary Bostick's youngest daughter, Martha.
³ Ibid.
⁴ Ibid.
⁵ Ibid. Attie refers to G. P. as "Papa" in this letter.
⁶ Attie Bostick to Bertha Bostick, January 6, 1916.

enjoyed it. Indeed, I'd love to have made one of those 'women's party,' but I really had a happy Christmas here. It certainly makes a great difference having children here." Attie's cats, however, did not appreciate the children's visit: "Kitty normally lies on my warm hand day and night, but she cleared their deck when Wade and Oreon came. She didn't give them half a chance to make friends with her and Ponto was afraid of Wade's crutches!"[7]

Despite having a pleasant time with her brother's family at Christmas, Attie hinted to Bertha about being a little homesick: "I'd love to walk with you in those woods, and I'd love to live there for several months. I think I'm not planning to go home this year," for she had too much work and too few funds. Nevertheless, "time *flies* by and it will probably not be many more years till I find a way to go."[8] Indeed, Attie would return home on furlough in two and a half years.

Attie's Application to the Southern Baptist Foreign Mission Board
After much prayer, Attie finally decided in March 1916 to apply to the Southern Baptist FMB. Having served as a Gospel Mission missionary for almost sixteen years, Attie, now forty years old, agonized over leaving the program, but she eventually determined that she should change mission programs. She submitted the following application letter to the FMB:

Dear Brethren:

Having worked in China since June 16, 1900, as a member of the Gospel Mission, and now feeling convinced that I can better serve God in connection with the Southern Baptist Convention, I desire to present to your Board my application to be appointed as a regular missionary for the Southern Baptist Convention. It is with the full approval of my workers in the Gospel Mission, Rev. and Mrs. T. L. Blalock, with whom I have labored in the closest harmony and fellowship these years, that I present this application with the earnest request from them, that I be allowed to continue in this field [Taian] and that just as soon as the Lord gives the means to send forth these laborers, you send others to help in this needy field.

---

[7] Ibid. Attie's nephew Wade perhaps had broken his leg or ankle. See Attie Bostick to Adelaide Bostick, January 6, 1916.
[8] Attie Bostick to Bertha Bostick, January 6, 1916.

Should you be led of God to accept my application, I am hopeful that the First Church, Gastonia, N.C., will undertake my full support and shall try to encourage them to do so. They sent me out as a Gospel Missionary and practically supported me the first seven years I was out here, but later dropped me to work in connection with the regular organized work.

Trusting to hear from you at your earliest convenience and praying God to direct you in this and all matters to His glory.

I am, Most Sincerely,
Attie T. Bostick[9]

Edgar L. Morgan, a Southern Baptist missionary who had met Attie in Taian, wrote a reference letter on her behalf to the FMB's foreign secretary, T. Bronson (T. B.) Ray.[10] Morgan described Attie as "a remarkably fine woman, a worker equal to any of our ladies under the Board, and I wish to commend her heartily to your attention. The circumstances seem to favor her entrance into that field, and no better way can be found than to continue these workers who are now there. I hope she will be appointed."[11]

In response to her application letter, Ray sent Attie an application form and a certificate to be completed by her physician, indicating the condition of her health. In her letter of May 30, 1916, Attie apologized to Ray for not sending anything from

"Attie T. Bostick, Taianfu, Shantung, China. Feb.1916, 160 lbs."—Attie Bostick

---

[9] Attie Bostick to the Southern Baptist Foreign Mission Board, March 13, 1916.
[10] After Robert J. Willingham died in 1914, J. Franklin Love succeeded him as corresponding secretary and the Southern Baptist Convention added another secretary position at the Foreign Mission Board, the foreign secretary, which was filled by T. B. Ray.
[11] Edgar L. Morgan to T. B. Ray, April 22, 1916, in the League, Attie T. Bostick folder, Foreign Mission Board Correspondence Collection (FMBCC), Box 33, Southern Baptist Historical Library and Archives (SBHLA), Nashville, TN.

her physician in her first letter, "but having stood the climatic changes these sixteen years and being in robust health, I just naturally took it for granted that would be my recommendation as to health while of course, you know nothing of my state of health."[12]

Attie informed Ray that she hoped "to attend the Baptist Conference in Chefoo next month (beginning June 22nd) and several of the East Shantung missionaries had expressed the hope that they might be able to welcome me at their mission meeting, just after, as a member of their mission." She also mentioned a situation that worried Southern Baptist missionaries throughout the world—debt. "I am very anxious to hear the Board is out of debt, and await anxiously news from the convention, which met only seventy five miles from my old home. From my earliest recollections," she told Ray, "my sainted father taught me to hate and avoid debt and I feel it is greatly against our cause when there is a debt."[13] At that time the FMB was nearly $100,000 in debt.

Along with her letter to Ray, Attie probably sent her application form, which she had completed on May 24. She had answered several questions concerning her skills, calling, commitment to missions, and temperament, though some of the questions undoubtedly caused the sixteen-year-foreign missionary to smile:

Do you get along well with others? "Yes, I think I do."

Is your temperament such that you can easily adapt yourself to the new and strange conditions of life in a foreign field? "I have, I think, done so for 16 years."

What success have you had in personal efforts to bring others to Christ? "God has blessed my efforts in trying to lead others to Him."

How long have you entertained the desire to become a foreign missionary? "Since 1889 when Bro. G. P. preached a farewell sermon on, 'She hath done what she could.'"

Why do you wish to become a foreign missionary? "In obedience to my Savior's command in Matthew 28:19-20."[14]

---

[12] Attie Bostick to T. B. Ray, May 30, 1916.
[13] Ibid. See also Attie Bostick to T. B. Ray, January 4, 1923.
[14] Application for Appointment as Missionary, Foreign Mission Board, Southern Baptist Convention, [1, 3], in the League, Attie T. Bostick folder, FMBCC, Box 33, SBHLA.

Unfortunately, Attie learned that the FMB would not be able to support her because of its debt. In a letter in August, she explained to Ray the precarious position in which she now found herself: "I am in rather a peculiar situation–neither the Gospel Mission nor the Board claim me, but God has very lovingly supplied my needs for which I thank Him. Of course I consider myself belonging to the G. M. till I resign, but some of them are not willing to claim me since they have heard that I applied to work with the Board."[15]

Attie also described to Ray some of her recent work, noting that "Last week we closed a two week Bible Class at which there was an average attendance of about thirty and I think much help was gained from it. Four men were baptized."[16] She then discussed the difficulties several missionaries were having with some Gospel Mission missionaries. Attie's description of the tense situation is difficult to understand at some points, but apparently some missionaries had "gone into Pentecostalism." One of those missionaries, a Mr. Anglin, had also caused dissention because he had not been dividing the financial support equally among the missionaries who shared common supporters with him. Anglin's actions caused Attie to remark: "His methods and practices are harmful to the cause of missions in general and to our Baptist work in particular."[17]

Attie mentioned the turmoil because she thought that it could be turned into good:

> There is a member of Dr. John E. White's church in Anderson, SC that I have had much on my mind recently and have even felt to write and ask her to take me up and support me as her missionary. She is Miss V. D. Brown who has, I think, ever since G. M.s started, contributed to some of us. She fully supported ($450.00) Mrs. Anglin and at the same time gave something to four others in the G. M. I think she has discontinued Mrs. Anglin's support since they went into Pentecostalism though I am not certain for she [Miss Brown] was a little inclined toward Pentecostalism herself. But I think if she understood the situation here she would not continue to send to them. . . . I can't feel she would go on supporting them if she knew the real facts, and as I said, I am not sure she does anyway, but why do I write you this?
>
> Well, I know Miss Brown has all along, also contributed to the Board and I wondered if you might not at this time, get her sympathies fully enlisted. My thought was that you could forward this letter of mine to her

---

[15] Attie Bostick to T. B. Ray, August 8, 1916.
[16] Ibid.
[17] Ibid.

pastor, Dr. White, whom I once met . . . and let him do as he thinks best about speaking to Miss Brown. I have thought of writing her direct and I may later on, but I know she thinks the Blalocks and I were perhaps unfair to the Anglins and so my letter, direct to her, might have less effect than through her pastor when she hears that his old school mate and friend, Mr. Rushin, who came out here specially to help him [Anglin], has in less than two years found him so unfair, she may be more lenient toward the Blalocks and me and even wonder that we continued trying to work with him for nearly five years.[18]

Attie's lack of financial support from either the Gospel Mission plan or the Southern Baptist FMB, however, did not cause her to quit. By the grace of God, she continued to work in China.

Attie's Appointment by the Foreign Mission Board

Despite not being accepted by the FMB, Attie continued corresponding with Ray, offering suggestions about how the work in China might be done better and notifying him of her immediate plans. In one letter she informed Ray: "Next week I plan to go thirty miles out east to a village where we have had much to encourage us and where they say there are a great number now waiting for baptism. We plan to take our tent there and hold several days' meetings. Then I hope to get around to as many places as possible before the colder weather sets in and cuts me off from traveling and being in their fireless homes." Notwithstanding her precarious financial situation, Attie maintained a positive attitude, noting: "The weather is beautiful now and I am so thankful for good health to go about my Master's business."[19]

In October 1916 Attie finally received word that she had been appointed as a Southern Baptist missionary. Aiding her acceptance was the sacrifice of the Southern Baptist missionaries of the North China Mission, who offered to pay Attie's salary for six months. In a letter to Ray, she praised God for once again providing for her: "God has been good to me all my life in giving me warm earnest friends and I thank Him for this new love and care manifested by His children for me. It is my earnest desire to serve Him faithfully in this new relation I sustain to the Board, and my fellow missionaries here in China."[20]

Attie continued to care for the spiritual welfare of the Chinese and for the physical needs of her fellow missionaries. She nursed an English missionary, Sarah Townshend, during a six-month illness, and then helped Sarah care for her

---

[18] Ibid.
[19] Attie Bostick to T. B. Ray, September 22, 1916.
[20] Attie Bostick to T. B. Ray, November 28, 1916.

husband, Sidney, "with no physician attending through a bad spell of small pox."[21]

The Townshends had recently applied to the FMB, and Attie was interested in finding out from Ray about the status of their application. She recommended the Townshends "most heartily to the Board as most worthy and devout missionaries, ones who make you want to love more earnestly and prayerfully by just coming in contact with them." Sarah "came from a wealthy family in England where luxuries were enjoyed, but in the life she had out here, sometimes even necessities were not to be had, yet I never heard her murmur or complain, but was always cheery and plucky in it all. . . . I do hope the Board will be able to take them over. They are staunch Baptists."[22] The FMB appointed the Townshends in 1917, and they served in China until 1938.

Life in China often forced Attie to do things she had never done before. On the FMB's application form, Attie had written that she had no construction skills and that she hoped that she would never have to supervise the construction of a building. Life on the mission field, however, threw Attie another curve, and she reported to Ray that she was currently "looking after the repairing a house now, as my present landlord has given me notice that he must have the place I am now occupying for his use next year." She was "putting foreign windows and doors in a Chinese house" she was going to rent. Once again, Attie met an obstacle with a positive attitude: "It is quite a new experience for me and trying to hurry it before the freezing weather comes in. I have not been able to plan as I should have liked to for it. I suppose the experience will do me good though."[23]

Attie's appointment by the FMB enabled Southern Baptists to expand their North China Mission field to include a new station in Taian. The FMB previously had missionaries stationed in north China in Tungchow, Hwang-Hsien, Pingtu, Kiaochow, Laichow; and Lai Yang.[24] Taian, a city of 40,000, was an important mission area, for it was located at the foot of the most sacred mountain in China, Tai-Shan.[25] According to the Taoist religion, "Tai Shan rose from the head of Pangu, the creator of the

---

[21] Ibid.
[22] Ibid.
[23] Ibid.
[24] *Annual*, Southern Baptist Convention (SBC), 1902, 88; *Annual*, SBC, 1914, 194. Hwang-Hsien is now Huangcheng; Pingtu is now Pingdu; Kiaochow is now Jiaozhou; Laichow is now Laizhou; and Lai Yang is now Laiyang.
[25] *Annual*, SBC, 1918, 263.

world."²⁶ The town of Taian had the Dai Miao, a temple complex of more than 600 buildings where elaborate sacrifices were provided for the god of Tai Shan.

The year 1917, Attie's first full year with the FMB, proved to be difficult. Small pox broke out in five missionary schools, and a drought and floods devastated the year's crops. Moreover, World War I had also affected the Chinese in the north. Many of the Shantung merchants and coolies worked in neighboring Manchuria Province and in Siberia, using the Russian ruble notes for payment. With the collapse of Russia and the depreciation of the ruble, the Chinese experienced even more financial hardships.²⁷

Despite these the difficulties, Southern Baptist mission work continued in Shantung Province. The Taian area had "six churches, with a membership of nearly 400. One church was organized with a membership of 108."²⁸ The work with the Chinese women usually included separate Women's Chapels, in which services were held on Sundays and during the week. The women missionaries visited the Chinese women in their homes in both the city and the country. Attie and Laura Dawes taught classes in Taian and the surrounding area, and traveled to the outstations by wheelbarrow.²⁹

Attie's Furlough

In November 1918 Ray notified Attie that she had been granted a furlough. She wrote to Ray in January 1919, thanking him and providing him with her travel plans. G. P., who was still working in Pochow, made her traveling arrangements, thereby relieving her "of a great task. I have been fortunate the three times I have crossed the Pacific in having someone else do this for me each time so I am afraid I'm a bit spoiled."³⁰ Despite her need for a furlough, Attie was reluctant to leave because of her concern about the great amount of work needed to be done and the lack of a replacement for her. Nevertheless, an ambivalent Attie sailed for America in June 1919.

After an eleven-year absence from home, Attie finally returned to her "own, native land." She stopped first in Louisville, Kentucky, to visit her niece Adelaide, and then continued on to North Carolina to see her family and friends. Her joy in seeing the awe inspiring beauty of the Rockies and then ex-

---

²⁶ Tom Le Bas and Brian Bell, eds., *Insight Guides China* (Maspeth, NY: Langenscheidt Publishers, Inc., 2004), 173-74.
²⁷ *Annual*, SBC, 1918, 262-63. Tsar Nicholas II abdicated his throne on March 15, 1917, and was replaced by the ineffective Kerensky Provisional Government, which was overthrown by the Bolsheviks on November 7, 1917.
²⁸ Ibid., 264.
²⁹ Ibid., 267.
³⁰ Attie Bostick to T. B. Ray, January 14, 1919.

periencing the comfort, peace, and serenity of the woods of her beloved North Carolina allayed her reluctance to leave China.[31]

When Attie arrived in Shelby, North Carolina, her eighty-four-year-old mother was in declining health. The care of her mother had fallen on the shoulders of Attie's sister Judie, who was now fifty-eight and whose years of serving as their parents' caregiver had taxed her health. Judie had always functioned as the second mother of the family and had cared for her younger siblings when they were young. She had been the dutiful daughter who had not married, deciding to do what many daughters in the nineteenth-century did: remain in the family home to care for aging parents. Seeing that Judie needed help, Attie decided to care for her mother and to teach school at nearby Boiling Springs High School. Even while caring for her aging mother, the cause of missions remained with Attie. She sent her teacher's salary to the FMB to help repay its large debt.

The health of Attie's mother continued to deteriorate, and in her letter of December 9, 1919, Attie accepted Ray's suggestion that she extend her furlough. "I find it rather difficult to collect my thoughts in this busy hurrying America," she confessed, "and often find myself longing for the quiet slow ways of my dear adopted country." Consequently, she did not relish the prospect of extending her furlough: "I do not like to ask or expect favors and had meant to abide by the Board's rule of only one year in America but since you so kindly suggest that I stay through August I shall be glad to feel free to do so. I feel I have much to be thankful for—the good health I have enjoyed since my arrival though I have been very busy and have had practically no rest."[32]

As Attie prepared for her return to China in August 1920, Ray wrote to her about her travel plans. Attie wanted to sail from San Francisco, but the FMB could not do that for her. Ray hoped, however, "that the great company of friends going out will more than compensate for the loss of the privilege of sailing from San Francisco." He also discussed the purchase of Attie's ticket for her passage: "We are not expecting to send anyone second-class. All will go first-cabin. It is good for you to be willing to take second or even third class, but we feel we could not call upon anyone to do this. I will engage passage for you on the *Empress of Japan*, which is the ship we are to use for our large party."[33]

In two subsequent letters, Attie diplomatically attempted to convince Ray to purchase a second-class ticket for her. Nearly eleven years earlier, she had in-

---

[31] Attie Bostick to T. B. Ray and J. Franklin Love, July 22, 1919.
[32] Attie Bostick to T. B. Ray, December 9, 1919.
[33] T. B. Ray to Attie Bostick, March 23, 1920.

Jane Bostick and her daughter Judie Bostick, c. 1918

Standing back: Judie Bostick, Bertha Bostick
Seated front: Jane Bostick, Attie Bostick, c. 1919

Bostick Family, East Graham Street, Shelby, NC, January or February 1919
First row standing: (2nd left) Attie Bostick, Mary Bostick Austell, Judie Bostick, Louisa Bostick Putnam, G. P. Bostick, Lena Bostick, Sam Austell [note: Lena is last person in this row]
Seated center: Jane Suttle Bostick, and her brother, Dr. B. F. Suttle

formed R. J. Willingham, corresponding secretary of the FMB, about the virtues of traveling second class.[34] "If some Baptist friends who are thinking of going on the ship with us are not able to go First Cabin," she suggested to Ray,

> you will I suppose, allow me to go that way, as they have asked that I chaperone the party. I am not sure they will go on the *Empress of Japan*, or that they will not go first class, but I wanted to make this explanation in case I should later ask to go that way. I really would like to go that way any way. I'm a good sailor and Second Cabin is not bad. I hear rates have gone up so since we came home last year. We came on the *Empress of Japan*. The Tedders came Third Class on the *Russia* and liked it very well—They had gone over Second.[35]

A week later, still singing the praises of traveling second class, Attie informed Ray that she had found cheaper passage out of San Francisco: "I find I can engage passage, second cabin, on the *Nile*, sailing from San Francisco August 28 for $144.00. This is a large ship, 14000 tonnage. I went out second cabin on the *Minnesota* in 1908 and liked it very much. There were over fifty missionaries on with us and the roughest weather made very little difference on that large ship, and so there was not much seasickness."[36] Attie also preferred to leave in May, instead of August, but only if leaving earlier would not be a "financial loss" to the FMB. Explaining her strong desire to leave from San Francisco, she wrote that she had traveled to China twice before on different routes and wanted to take a different route.

The desire to experience something new, however, was not Attie's main reason for suggesting different traveling arrangements; rather, it was a matter of conscience. She explained her reasoning to Ray:

> First class on the same ship is $224, so I save $80.00 by going that way. I know something of the sacrifices made by some people who give to missions and I feel I'd be doing *wrong* to spend that much uselessly. I can save the Board that much and be just as comfortable and a great deal more happy than if I went first class on the *Empress of Japan*. I shall be sorry to miss our large party and even the delightful help of my own brother, unless he decides to change too, but there is a small party going on the *Nile*, going to Taian and I feel I can be more company and help to them than to the larger crowd. So please write me as soon as possible and let me know if it is all right that I go this way. I'm sure it is unless you have paid for my passage.[37]

---

[34] See Attie Bostick to R. J. Willingham, November 25, 1908, and above in Chapter Two.
[35] Attie Bostick to T. B. Ray, March 26, 1920.
[36] Attie Bostick to T. B. Ray, April 2, 1920.
[37] Ibid.

Attie's insistence on traveling second class was not some masochistic desire on her part; it was a matter of good stewardship. On her application form to the FMB in 1916, she had answered "Yes" to the question: "Will you practice strict economy in spending the money of the Board, remembering the sacrifices made by contributors?"[38] In her view, traveling second class was one tangible way of honoring those people who contributed to the cause of missions.

Attie did not return to China in May, as she had hoped, nor did she return in August. Because her mother's health continued to deteriorate, Attie felt that she was still needed at home. Her furlough was extended again, enabling Attie to care for her mother in her dying days. On October 23, 1921, with Attie and many family members at her bedside, Jane Suttle Bostick died a peaceful death.

In a letter eleven days later, Attie described her mother's last days to J. Franklin Love, who, in 1915, succeed Willingham as the FMB's corresponding secretary:

> You doubtless have heard of the Home going of my dear mother.... She was confined to her bed only one week. All trace of pain and suffering seemed to leave her face the last three days and it grew more radiant at the last. Her going was like a babe falling asleep – no struggle at all at the last. One of her former pastors, her nephew J. W. Suttle, said there was absolutely no sting to such a death and so we were comforted. We feel she is happy with Jesus, whom she declared three days before she left us she was believing in, and with her many loved ones who had gone on before, and whom she called the names of so often during her last illness. But oh how we miss her![39]

Attie's Preparation for Her Return to China

After her mother's death, and having spent two and a half years away from the mission field, Attie was eager to return to her beloved China. In her letter of November 3, 1921, to Love, in which she recounted her mother's death, Attie also notified the corresponding secretary that, although she was supposed to finish her teaching assignment in April 1922 at Boiling Springs High School, she could leave early. The school's principal, J. D. Huggins, whom Attie described as "one of the noblest Christian gentlemen I have ever known," supported her work as a missionary and would accommodate her desire to return to China as soon as possible.

While Attie was on furlough, the FMB closed its mission station in Taian, transferring it back to independent missionaries.[40] The Taian mission field was extremely large, covering approximately 100 square miles and containing

---

[38] Application for Appointment as Missionary, Foreign Mission Board, Southern Baptist Convention, [1].
[39] Attie Bostick to J. Franklin Love, November 3, 1921. Love served as corresponding secretary from 1915 to 1928.
[40] *Annual*, SBC, 1921, 321.

approximately 500 Christians.[41] When she returned to the United States on furlough in 1919, Attie and Laura and Joseph Dawes were the only FMB missionaries serving this large mission field.[42] In 1920, after Laura Dawes was diagnosed with a malignant tumor, she and her husband returned to America, and Frank and Mary Connely moved to Taian to take the Dawes's place. When the FMB closed its mission in Taian, the Connelys returned to Tsining, where they had served for several years.[43]

Attie asked for Love's opinion as to when and to what city she should return to in China. Her brother Wade and his wife had suggested that she finish teaching and then rest before returning. The Townshends had asked her to work with them in Kweiteh (now Shangqiu), Honan (now Hunan) Province, but she preferred to return to Taian, where she had served for ten years. "When I moved from Pochow to Taian," she explained, "I almost promised myself I'd never move again, in China, as I feel I lose in my work and influence by doing so. I think I am sure of what I say when I say the present Baptist workers would be glad to have me there, and I think, too, the Chinese would." Attie then alluded to some tension among the missionaries in Taian: "I feel I might, by the Spirit's blessing, be used to reunite where there has been division."[44]

Before ending her letter, Attie empathized with Love for "having to retrench" because of the FMB's ever-growing debt. She expressed her exasperation with the debt and with what she considered to be its cause: "I wish our Baptist people would work and not play at the great work of foreign missions. I do hope there will be no debt next spring."[45] Her hope, however, would not be fulfilled. The debt eventually rose above $1 million and would not be eradicated for another twenty-two years.[46]

In response, Love conveyed his condolences and advised Attie to "return to China and abide [by] the decision of the Mission as to where you shall be permanently located. If the Mission acts before you reach China, then, of course, you will govern yourself accordingly. Perhaps, a short stay in Taian might help you to re-establish such relations between the workers there and our Southern

---

[41] *Annual*, SBC, 1920, 277.
[42] *Annual*, SBC, 1919, 246.
[43] *Annual*, SBC, 1920, 277; *Annual*, SBC, 1921, 321.
[44] Attie Bostick to J. Franklin Love, November 3, 1921. See also Attie Bostick to J. Franklin Love, April 19, 1922.
[45] Attie Bostick to J. Franklin Love, November 3, 1921.
[46] See William R. Estep, *Whole Gospel—Whole World: The Foreign Mission Board of the Southern Baptist Convention, 1845-1995* (Nashville: Broadman & Holman Publishers, 1994), 208, 221, 225-26.

Baptist forces in Shantung as would be to the interest and advancement of that which we are all trying to do."[47]

Love then addressed the tension to which Attie had alluded in her letter: "I have heard rumors of some things which indicate that since Brother Blalock's return there has developed an attitude which I did not feel existed when I saw him. I have nothing very definite and, perhaps, nothing has happened which mars the relationship, but if such has, then you can, perhaps, render a distinct service upon your return."[48] Blalock served with the Gospel Mission program, and, unfortunately, the nature of his "attitude" is unknown. Obviously, he and other missionaries were not getting along. In a subsequent letter to Love, however, Attie was reluctant to put the blame of the dissention completely on Blalock.[49]

Although she desired to return to Taian, Attie put the matter in God's hands. Her primary desire, she declared to Love, was to seek "God's guidance as to when I shall return and where I shall return and where He will have me settle." Attie hoped that no decision would be made concerning her place of service until she arrived back in China because she wanted to have a say in where she served and "to be as certain" as she could be about God's "leading in the matter." Yet she also did not "want to be the cause of any dissention."[50]

After spending two and a half years on furlough, Attie returned to an uncertain future in China, having suffered the loss of her mother and the loss of her place of service in Taian. She admitted that she did not "like moving and readjustments," yet she also understood that such obstacles "must come in this life and I cannot get back to my work in China without these, so I hope day by day to be led aright."[51] Thus, on January 10, 1922, Attie began her journey back to China and to a new field of service.

---

[47] J. Franklin Love to Attie Bostick, November 9, 1921.
[48] Ibid.
[49] Attie Bostick to J. Franklin Love, November 12, 1921.
[50] Ibid.
[51] Attie Bostick to J. Franklin Love, November 20, 1921.

Chapter Four

ATTIE'S MINISTRY DURING POLITICAL UNREST
1922-1929

For I was an hungred, and ye gave me meat: I was thirsty, and ye gave me drink: I was a stranger, and ye took me in: Naked, and ye clothed me: I was sick, and ye visited me: I was in prison, and ye came unto me. . . . Inasmuch as ye have done it unto one of the least of these my brethren, ye have done it unto me. (Matt. 25:35-36, 40)

"Mr. and Mrs. League and I just outside of their flower house. Feb. 1922"—Attie Bostick

Attie's Return to a Starving and Dangerous China

After arriving back in China, Attie first traveled to Taian to assess the problems there. In November 1921, Dr. Love had asked her to make a short stay there to help reestablish the relationship between the Gospel Mission missionaries in Taian and the Southern Baptist missionaries.[1] She found that there were two factions among the Chinese, and the dissention hindered the mission work.[2] Attie's visit to Taian allowed her to reunite with her old friends T.J. and Florence League. While visiting with the Leagues, Attie took numerous pictures that she sent to her family. One of the photographs shows her standing on Frog Mountain at Tai Shan.

When Attie returned to China, the country was suffering from a famine and civil unrest. The famine started early in 1921 and was followed later that autumn by massive floods that destroyed the fall crops. In her report on the Interior China Mission, Mary Braun described the devastation of these natural disasters for Southern Baptists back home:

> The year 1921 opened with one of the most bitter famines in history. . . . Many of our missionaries gave most of their time to relief work and the stories of their experiences with *starving* people will never be completely told.

---
[1] J. Franklin Love to Attie Bostick, November 9, 1921.
[2] Attie Bostick to J. Franklin Love, April 19, 1922.

"Mr. and Mrs. T. J. League on Tai San."
—Attie Bostick, c. 1922

"Mrs. League's flower house. Feb. 1922"
—Attie Bostick

"Mrs. League holding her kittens. (I've agreed to take one home with me) at the north west corner …bedroom window…"—Attie Bostick

Attie Bostick, c. 1922

"The Frog Mt. on Taishan—1922"
—Attie Bostick

Then, during the summer months, while the famine was still preying upon the life of north and central China, the lands were deluged with floods of rain. Two years of rain was poured out on six weeks' time and literally the earth could not contain it. Thousands of homes were destroyed. Crops, so essential after a year of famine, did not yield even the seed that was planted. Famine, flood, and more famine therefore, form the background picture for this year's work. The people at home were liberal in sending out money for relief. The International Famine Committee for Honan [Province] . . . distributed millions of dollars of grain and copper coins, while our own executive committee carefully expended the famine money sent to this mission through the Foreign Mission Board.[3]

After her visit to Taian, Attie spent nearly a month with her brother G. P. and his family in Pochow. G. P. had organized a famine relief effort there, and most of his time was spent dispensing aid. In a letter to his daughter Bertha, he described the hectic and perilous situation in his mission field:

"This wasn't properly focused, but you can see the swollen faces of those three beggars-not just famine poor. They ate tree leaves & were poisoned from them This is one place where we gave funds out to them."– Attie Bostick c. 1922

> I have been in a perfect whirl for a month. . . . We distributed grain last Saturday to 1500 families and got through very well. There are some 1,000 or more people at work now on roads and a river that I am supposed to overlook in a general way. It is "all plenty" to do. . . People are starving around us in spite of all that can be done! Out there is a fine prospect for a full wheat crop. But it may be cut very short by drought and dry wind.[4]

"Mr. Bostick at a tea house on the road to the great sacred mountain, Tai Shan."— Lena Bostick, c. 1922

G. P. also wrote that everyone had enjoyed seeing Attie, "especially her old Chinese friends." Her time in Pochow, however, was more than a social call, for she had assisted in the distribution of grain.[5]

---

[3] *Annual*, Southern Baptist Convention (SBC), 1922, 258. See also Edgar L. Morgan's report for the North China Mission, ibid., 264.
[4] G. P. Bostick to Bertha Bostick, April, 19, 1922.
[5] Ibid.

"This was one of the ruins taken the next day after the looting & burning of this city but it doesn't show up very well. About 300 rooms were burned."
—Attie Bostick, c. 1922

After visiting the Bosticks in Pochow, Attie traveled to her new station in Kweiteh. Upon her return to China, she had accepted Sarah and Sidney Townshend's appeal to join them in their work. Attie's presence "greatly strengthened and encouraged" the Townshends, who had served in Kweiteh for several years as the only missionaries.[6] A few days after Attie's arrival in Kweiteh, the city erupted in violence. On April 17, 1922, soldiers looted the city and burned several stores. Attie described the dangerous situation to J. Franklin Love: "Many guns were fired by both parties and we, being near the east gate, were very near some of the bullets as they whistled by, but God kept us, unmolested. Two stores right in front of us were sacked completely." Miraculously, the looters did not harm the Southern Baptist missionaries. The gatekeeper of Attie's home overheard some of the looters say, "Don't bother them. They have saved so many people's lives," a reference to the missionaries' help during the famine. Other people in the city were not so fortunate: "Several men were shot in the looting and three of them were not dead when Mr. and Mrs. Townshend and I went on the street about nine o'clock yesterday

---

[6] *Annual*, SBC, 1923, 72.

morning yet hundreds were passing them by and doing nothing at all for them. We had them carried to the hospital but it was too late. These dead, two of them were just carried outside the city wall and thrown down for the dogs and crows to feast on, right in sight of our place!"[7]

Despite the fighting, by the autumn of 1922 all of the outstations of the Kweiteh station had been visited, which included a three or four days' meeting conducted by Attie and a native evangelist, Mr. Tung, at each outstation. In her report for the Interior China Mission to the Foreign Mission Board (FMB), Zemma Hare highlighted the fruit of such meetings: "At least one thousand women have heard the gospel and the attendance and interest on the part of the Christians have been very marked.

"Mr. & Mrs. Townshend and my pets in their arms. Aren't they pretty? The pets & the Ts are just as nice & kind to me & my pets as can be. I thought kitty was lost or stolen today, but she came home ... a little before sundown, & I was glad to see her."—Attie Bostick, c. 1922

Christian women have left their homes and gone with Miss Bostick testifying of what Jesus has done for them and could do for others. There have been circulated 10,429 Gospels and portions of the Scriptures, besides many New Testaments and thousands of tracts."[8] Attie had also helped Sarah and Sidney Townshend in the mission school, teaching the forty-two boys and forty girls Bible stories and how to sing.

Just before Christmas 1922, Attie received a welcome gift from friends—money to purchase a Ford. The car would enable the Kweiteh missionaries to visit the outstations more easily, "even if we are not allowed to spend the night. This will increase our ability to visit and witness very much and we are most grateful for it."[9] The days of traveling by wheelbarrow were thankfully over.

Also in December 1922 Attie traveled to Pochow to spend Christmas with her brothers Wade and G. P. and their families. Wade had built a new home and three school buildings for the educational complex. Attie loved her brother's new home, describing it as "better than any I've ever seen in China. It is comfortable and home-like, but I suppose it is the location that appeals

---

[7] Attie Bostick to J. Franklin Love, April 19, 1922.
[8] *Annual*, SBC, 1923, 72.
[9] Attie Bostick to T. B. Ray, January 4, 1923.

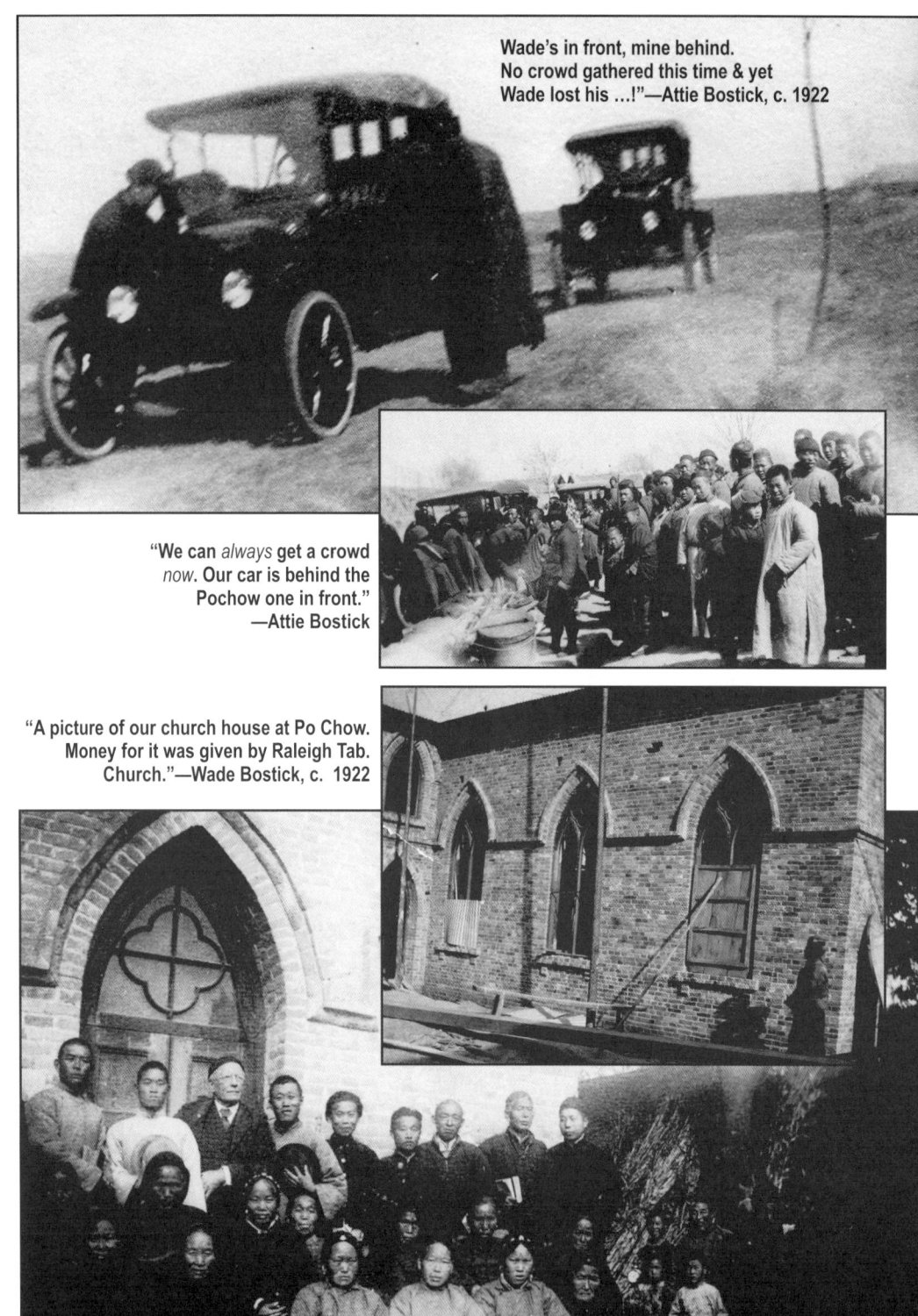

"Wade's in front, mine behind. No crowd gathered this time & yet Wade lost his ...!"—Attie Bostick, c. 1922

"We can *always* get a crowd now. Our car is behind the Pochow one in front."
—Attie Bostick

"A picture of our church house at Po Chow. Money for it was given by Raleigh Tab. Church."—Wade Bostick, c. 1922

"Wade & part of the 32 he baptized on Nov. Some got left out at the left. Those two children & the ones behind them do not belong in."—Attie Bostick, c. 1922

to me most—no wall between it and the river, but a wire fence so we can see up and down the river and the tints at sunrise and sunset are beautiful. His school buildings are sensible and well adapted for the use of boys desirous of any education and willing to work some toward that end."[10]

"Wade's new home, facing south with no wall or obstruction between them & with out a wire fence." —Attie Bostick, c. 1922

[No picture] "Don't think it must have cost 'thousands.' It is comfortably furnished all within $1,000 (US money)."—Attie Bostick, c. 1922

"Wade's mt. house. I'll let these pictures be my letter this time. Lots of love to all. Attie" c. 1922

"The lower is our new house taken across the valley. The house faces south & Wade had his room off the porch. Stone was blasted off the side for building."
—Attie Bostick

"Cousin Blanche Walker, our cook, & his wife on the east near Wade's bedroom window."—Attie Bostick, c. 1922

"The west side of the new house on Mt.—my bedroom—Miss Walker's (middle) & the servants (marked)."
—Attie Bostick, c. 1922

[10] Ibid.

Attie's Rebuke of the Foreign Mission Board

Soon after returning to Kweiteh from Pochow, Attie wrote to the FMB's foreign secretary, T. B. Ray, admonishing the board for its insensitive treatment of Mary Lawton, a single woman missionary who had applied to work in Kaifeng, near her missionary parents, Deaver and Dorothy Lawton. Despite Lawton's request, the FMB assigned her to Hwang-Hsien, Shantung Province, 400 miles from her parents in Chenhchow, Honan Province.[11]

In her letter to Ray, Attie emphasized her foreign mission experience and her personal knowledge of Mary Lawton. Attie's experience contrasted sharply with Ray's lack of actual mission experience and his incomplete understanding of Lawton's opinion concerning her appointment. Attie reminded Ray that in a previous letter to him about Lawton, she had based her comments on her "23 years as a single lady missionary out here and I felt where it was possible for a single lady to live with her parents and still be just as efficient a missionary, it was best that she do so. It would seem the natural thing to the Chinese who know her and her parents, and there would be ample opportunity for her to work on her own initiative too. She could be a help to her parents, in the work and they to her." Mary had informed Ray that she and her parents had accepted the FMB's decision. Once again, however, Attie spoke from personal knowledge: "Yes, I think Mary and her parents have both been very sweet-spirited in the matter and have conceded to your decision in an excellent spirit, but I happened to travel with Mary as she went to Hwanghsien and I heard her say it had almost made her doubt her call to the mission field, . . . so you see it was not as easy as it may have seemed in her letter to you."[12]

Attie's rebuke continued: "The unBaptistic part to me is that you did not send her to the place she requested to go to and if I understand correctly the mission at Kaifeng and Hwanghsien both agreed with her in that request." If acting unBaptist was not enough to shame the FMB, Attie noted that the board had not risen to the compassion and wisdom with which the Canadian and Lutheran missions treated their missionaries, observing "that they leave the settling of the individual missionary to the missionary concerned and to the ones already out here. That is the way you did me. You said consult with the missionaries out here and decide the matter."[13]

In yet another rebuke, Attie highlighted the insensitivity of the FMB's decision: "I know she will likely see her parents a great deal more than the average

---
[11] Hwang-Hsien is now Huangcheng. Chenhchow is now Chenzhou.
[12] Attie Bostick to T. B. Ray, January 4, 1923.
[13] Ibid.

missionary, but she was deprived of them in her school days in a way that many of us were not, but really that is not my first argument or main point in it, at all. I feel she could make a far better missionary and exert a greater influence over the Chinese in working from her parent's home."[14]

Although her remarks seem to indicate otherwise, Attie assured Ray that she was not trying to convince the FMB to change its decision concerning Lawson's assignment; rather, she merely "wanted to explain my position more clearly to you."[15] After reading the letter, Ray undoubtedly knew Attie's position on the matter.

Attie's Financial Support of Needy Chinese Girls

Several of Attie's 1923 letters referred to her financial support of some needy Chinese girls. Walter Cowery, the superintendent of the Hill-Murray Institute for the Blind, described the progress of a little blind girl whom Attie had taken to Peking:

> Your girl is getting along quite nicely. She has settled down wonderfully well, and she seems to enjoy the life. She has begun learning Braille Characters and she is learning how the numerals are formed, [and is about] ready for using the arithmetic frame. They have started to teach her simple knitting with needles, and also how to use a knitting frame. Altogether I think they manage to keep her busy, and the busier she gets the happier she will be, at least that is the usual experience. It's easy to bring a smile on her face, and that I think suggests that she is now settled.[16]

"'Poinger' and her little two months old son. She & her husband [were] in a Bible Class at Kaifeng."—Attie Bostick, c. 1923

In a postscript to a letter addressed to "Loved Ones," Attie asked her brother Wade in Pochow to pay $4.00 on a little girl's account.[17] To her sister Judie, Attie noted happily that "My girl is in school . . . and improving."[18] Attie kept her sister informed about the status of other children she was helping. After attending a meeting in Kaifeng, Attie

---

[14] Ibid.
[15] Ibid.
[16] Walter Cowery to Attie Bostick, May 10, 1923.
[17] Attie Bostick to Loved Ones, October 10, 1923.
[18] Attie Bostick to Judie Bostick, November 7, 1923.

brought home one of our girls who had gone up there to school. She had typhoid and double pneumonia and now has T. B. They say she is so thin and wasted away, it is pitiful. As the train left Kaifeng that day she broke down and cried and asked if there would be any one at the train to meet us and I told her yes, and for her not to bother as I look after everything. She had to be carried and cared for like a baby. Later I was talking with her and asked her if God should not heal her but call her away would she like it and with the brightest of smiles she said she would. I told her there would be no doubt of someone meeting us when we got to our eternal Home. Yesterday she was put on a barrow and taken to her home about eight miles in the country, and I hope she stood the trip all right. I offered to put her in the hospital here and pay her expenses, but she wanted to go home, though. It won't be ready or clean nor will she get as good things to eat, but "there's no place like home" to them, too.[19]

"Your adopted daughter in Christ."
— Sr. Dolores of S. H. J., c. 1923

Because of her ministry to several needy children, Attie apparently had received some kidding about becoming an adopted mother and starting an orphanage. Attie good-naturedly assured her favorite sister Judie and her niece Bertha that she had done neither: "I pay for the blind girl's schooling, but her parents are living and still claim her. We hope she can make her own living after some years in school, as they learn to knit and weave there."[20] Although Attie had not started an orphanage, she admitted wanting to do so for a long time. She longed "to help the many needy girls I meet and hear of. I was in the country last week and ate a meal going and coming with the blind girl's parents and they seem

---

[19] Attie Bostick to Judie Bostick, November 4, 1923.
[20] Attie Bostick to Judie Bostick and Bertha Bostick, November 23, 1923.

"My little girl's mum & ..."
—Attie Bostick, c. 1932

very grateful for what I am doing for her. I pay $25.00 a year to keep her in school and they clothe her. Then I keep three girls in" a school in Pochow, "but pay only $16.00 a school term for them all, as they work for part of their time.[21]

Political Unrest

In 1923 the mission station at Kweiteh opened a new church building and ordained its first church officers—Mr. Dong Si Ming as pastor and Mr. Fang Long Kih as deacon. The light, airy church had seating capacity for 600, and a gallery when needed. As part of the goal to become self supporting, the Chinese had given over $600 of the $750 allotted them. Two new outstations were

"Our first congregation-at the temple given us for a meeting place. There's a "+" on my hat."—Attie Bostick, c. 1923

---

[21] Attie Bostick to Judie Bostick, December 1, 1923.

added with these funds. Over 15,000 Gospels and Scripture portions were sold, which was over 5,000 more than in 1922.[22]

As the Kweiteh ministry continued to expand, Attie hoped that the gospel seeds were falling on fertile ground. Attie wrote to Bertha: "I have been to church and Sunday School this morning. We had the temperance lesson. I meet with the R.A.'s [Royal Auxiliary] at 4:30 and then we have [a] meeting tonight. We have large congregations now and I hope the seed is falling on good ground and will bring forth fruit in the Salvation of souls. We are to have our meeting beginning on the14th."[23]

Despite the growth of the interest in the gospel, the political conditions grew worse in China. Sun Yat-sen, a Chinese Christian living in exile, was the intellectual leader and fund raiser of the Chinese Revolution. He and his followers helped to bring about the collapse of the Qing dynasty. After the Qing dynasty lost control of many provinces in 1911, the Chinese emperor called on Yuan Shikai, a military commander, to aid him in re-conquering rebel provinces. However, Yuan forced the emperor to abdicate. Between 1912 and his death in March 1916, Yuan ruled China first as a president and then as a self-declared emperor. Near the end of Yuan's life, his empire had begun to crumble because of the opposition of some military leaders. Following his death, the central government collapsed, and from 1916 until 1928 warlords ruled China. By 1924 five warlords ruled China, which helped stabilize the country. One of the warlords was General Feng Yu Hsiang (later Yuxiang).

General Feng, who had become a Christian in 1914, ruled Kweiteh and all of Honan Province. He did not drink, smoke, take opium, gamble, or chase women. He also forbad his troops to drink, swear, gamble, or visit prostitutes.[24] Known as the Christian General, Feng provided protection for the missionaries, but following his departure in 1924 to occupy Peking, another army led by the warlord Lao Yang Ren occupied areas of Honan Province, including Kweiteh. Ren, "the notorious . . . bandit chief," and "other ex-bandits did as they pleased and no one was safe. For six months" the missionaries in the China interior did not dare "to go out itinerating lest" they "be kidnapped and held for ransom."[25] In a letter to her sister Judie, Attie wrote that some missionary women who had been captured were released. Unfortunately, she did not provide the women's names, their places of service, or the circumstances

---

[22] *Annual*, SBC, 1924, 237.
[23] Attie Bostick to Bertha Bostick, November 4, 1923.
[24] J. A. G. Roberts, *A Concise History of China* (Cambridge, MA: Harvard University Press, 1999), 219.
[25] *Annual*, SBC, 1924, 237.

surrounding their kidnapping. Despite the danger, Attie still wanted to travel to the outstations to do the work that she loved: "I do long to put in all the time I can in helping others and my desire is that my life may be fruitful for Him who loved me and gave His life for me, with Paul I want and say 'Forgetting the past I press forward toward the mark of a higher calling in Christ Jesus'" [Phil. 3:14].[26]

Attie tried to assuage Judie's fears by explaining that she was living with the Townshends in Kweiteh. She reassured her sister that she got "plenty of good nourishing food, but I think I had plenty of that when I lived alone at Taian too. I guess I don't economize on that as much as you think I do on the dress question, for I feel it is a duty to keep my body well nourished and I had a good cook there too, who looks after my food well."[27]

By the end of November 1923 Attie felt that conditions were safe enough for her to travel again outside of Kweiteh. She also informed Judie and Bertha that the wife of the mission's Chinese evangelist who had been wounded was recovering, but the details surrounding the shooting of the woman are unknown. "She can walk," Attie noted thankfully, "but there is a little of the wound to heal yet. She applied for baptism, but cannot answer the questions satisfactorily, so she was asked to wait. She's very bashful and timid and I suppose will always be interested but embarrassed. She is pretty and I think is a Christian. She persecuted her husband when he first believed."[28]

"The window of sitting room facing south. I'm by bay window & Mrs. League by bathroom. The cane over which I cover mats in summer for a porch."—Attie Bostick, c. 1923

---

[26] Attie Bostick to Judie Bostick, November 4, 1923.
[27] Attie Bostick to Judie Bostick, November 7, 1923.
[28] Attie Bostick to Judie Bostick and Bertha Bostick, November 23, 1923.

"Women washing clothes at the corner of the city wall near us. It would be pretty enlarged."
—Attie Bostick, c. 1923

"Berfy, I got this from our upstairs north window. The large wall in the distance is the city wall, then water in the moat & a small fishing boat on it & green cane on the edge– the small wall encloses our garden."
—Attie Bostick, c. 1923

Despite living and working in dangerous circumstances, Attie found time to enjoy herself. Her letters during 1923 include information about things that women in much safer environments would talk about, such as Halloween, weddings, women bobbing their hair, clothes, and magazines.[29]

Success Stories from the Kweiteh Mission

In her 1924 report to the FMB, Attie recounted three success stories at the Kweiteh Mission. She described the conversion of a homeless, deaf mute man who lived in a temple. "'The deaf shall hear,' has a new meaning to me now," Attie began her report, "not that I have seen a miracle performed on the physical ears of anyone, but I feel I have seen even a greater miracle than this. Among the forty-seven men and women just recently baptized was a deaf mute, fifty years of age, and I feel he has heard the wooings of Spirit and is a child of God." Some of the man's family had already become Christians, and whenever the missionaries visited his town, "he was among the first to greet us and was always ready to help moving benches, going for water or in any way he could. How he learned it I do not know, but he did learn there was only one True God and he was right ready to tear down the idols and throw them

---

[29] See ibid., and Attie Bostick to Bertha Bostick, November 4, 1923.

out, but of course the elders of the town who did not believe in the True God stopped him before he had done more than disfigure one of the idol's hands." When the man presented himself before the church in his town to be examined before being baptized, "his face shown with joy as he answered the questions put to him in signs by the evangelist, and though he may never be able to sing with his tongue, I believe he will someday join in singing praises to Christ our Redeemer."[30]

Another success story involved Sister Yang, a seventy-two-year-old convert who, despite her age, had begun learning to read the previous year and was now able to read some passages of scripture and some Christian literature. Attie noted with joy that Yang's "face lights up with joy when she can meet together with us and learn a little more."[31]

The third success story involved the youngest, most recent convert, a twenty-one-year-old woman whose grandmother had been a Christian for several years. The young woman had given "a happy experience and seemed so happy in being able to be baptized along with the others." Her husband was not a believer and "got angry with her as soon as she came back from the baptizing and said she had to go home immediately." The missionaries, however, wanted the woman to stay so that she could participate in the Lord's Supper that afternoon. They also feared that if the woman returned home with her husband while "he was so angry he would probably beat her, and make it very hard for her."[32] Fortunately, the man permitted his wife to stay for the afternoon service.

More Political Unrest

The Southern Baptist missionary staff in Kweiteh in 1924 consisted of Attie and the Townshends, who were planning a furlough for 1925. During November and December 1924, Attie assisted Dr. Mary King, who was recuperating from surgery in Pochow. With the anticipated departure of the Townshends, two Chinese evangelists and their wives returned to Kweiteh from the Bible School at Kaifeng and were sent to outstations. The local churches there agreed to help support the evangelists financially, with the hope that those churches would provide total support in the future. A new church was completed in 1924 in Kweiteh, and the congregation was able to host the annual Honan-Anhwei Baptist Association in its new accom-

---

[30] Attie Bostick, "Report to the Foreign Mission Board on Interior China Mission, Kweiteh, China," April 23, 1924, in the League, Attie T. Bostick folder, Foreign Mission Board Correspondence Collection (FMBCC), Box 33, Southern Baptist Historical Library and Archives (SBHLA), Nashville, TN.
[31] Ibid.
[32] Ibid.

"This is the station building at the R.R. Mr. & Mrs. Townshend are the foreigners. I got this the day I went down to see the Herrings ..."—Attie Bostick, c. 1924

modations. Two new outstations were opened and supported completely by Chinese Christians. Also, a temple was donated for meetings at another outstation.[33]

In 1925 strong anti-foreign and anti-Christian sentiment emerged once again in China, which affected the missionaries' plans and programs. The anti-foreign sentiments gradually decreased during the year, and a large anti-Christian campaign that had been planned for Christmas day failed to materialize.[34]

The Townshends took their furlough in 1925, leaving Attie for much of the year as the only missionary in Kweiteh. She and the Chinese Christians continued the evangelistic work. In February they went house to house, inviting people to attend evangelistic services. These visits eventually resulted in new converts. Attie and Pastor Dong, a Chinese evangelist and the leader of the Chinese Christians in Kweiteh, visited the eleven outstations for three days each, at least once during 1925.[35] In September 1925 Attie received some much-needed help when Phillip and Mattie Macon White joined her at Kweiteh.[36]

Fighting in the interior, however, interrupted the evangelistic work. Lena Bostick, in her 1926 report on the Interior China Mission, described the situation:

---

[33] *Annual*, SBC, 1925, 240.
[34] *Annual*, SBC, 1926, 208.
[35] Ibid., 210-11.
[36] *Annual*, SBC, 1926, 211.

In mid-summer when local conditions were at their worst and leaders of the revolt were trying by persuasion and coercion to draw dividing lines, calling one side patriots and the other traitors, Pastor Dong was approached a number of times and begged to align himself with the 'patriots.' He steadfastly refused, knowing that such a step would mean disloyalty to God and Christianity. A more real test of fidelity came in the form of an invitation to become a preacher in General Feng's army, several times doubling his present salary. That he was able to put it behind him took nothing short of divine power and grace.[37]

In 1926, following the Chinese New Year, the missionaries and the Chinese Christians held a week of evangelistic services. They pitched tents at public fairs and festivals, and many people attended the five-hour worship services.[38] In the late spring the missionaries were unable to travel to the outstations due to bandits and the military conflict, but Attie and Pastor Dong eventually visited all of the outstations.[39] The Townshends returned in August from their furlough, providing much needed relief.

In mid-1926 Attie, her brother G. P., and thirty Chinese Christians helped organize the First Baptist Church in Hsuchow (now Xuchang), 110 miles southwest of Kweiteh, in Honan Province.[40] Fighting, however, continued to affect mission work, as Annie Sallee noted, "churches, schools, hospitals, homes, and religious work of every kind have been hindered, and in some instances completely wrecked by war, solders and bandits during the year 1926."[41] Attie wrote to her brothers G. P. and Wade about the effect of fighting on the family of the mission's Chinese evangelist, Mr. Dong. His brother had not been heard from and was believed to be killed by the Chinese solders or forced to serve in their army. Attie also described how some inexperienced Chinese solders were used as human shields during combat.[42]

Despite the political unrest caused by the numerous Chinese civil wars, Attie's work in rural China continued to be fruitful and rewarding. Attie wrote to Judie that when she traveled outside of Kweiteh, "I feel there is so much interest and so much needing doing that I'll just have to arrange to have weeks out and yet I am needed at home some too. . . . There is good interest and much to encourage every way."[43]

---

[37] Ibid., 210.
[38] *Annual*, SBC, 1927, 216.
[39] Ibid.
[40] Ibid., 218.
[41] Ibid., 215.
[42] Attie Bostick to G. P. Bostick and Wade Bostick, March 9, 1926.
[43] Attie Bostick to Judie Bostick, April 22, 1926.

The Death of G. P. Bostick

On June 22, 1926, Attie wrote to G. P.'s children, notifying them that their father had died:

> My precious Children,
>
> It is with the saddest of feelings that I begin this letter to take to you the news that you are doubly orphaned. Your father quietly drew his last breath in the Canadian hospital here [in Kweiteh] yesterday morning at nine o'clock and left to be with his Savior whom he loved and served so faithfully during his days here. The doctors and nurses were as kind as could be and we had an extra doctor from Kaifeng, but so far the medical world is baffled by this awful disease, typhus—there being no cure for it; and as I lay awake last night thinking what a work it wrought in his strong healthy body in so short a time, I prayed, Sam [G. P.'s son], that you might be among the doctors who shall later discover a remedy for this disease.[44]

G. P. had become sick on his return trip from visiting his daughter Mattie and her family in Tientsin (now Tianjin), Tianjin Province (now Tianjin). He had to change trains several times, and at the Tsinan (now Jinan) Station, he had to sleep on the floor "among a large number of soldiers, one of whom took the overcoat you had given him, Mattie, and appropriated it for a pillow." When G. P. discovered that his coat was missing, he found the soldier, asked him "what he was doing with his overcoat and got it back." Tragically, however, the soldier had infected the coat with typhus germs, which then were transferred to G. P.

Despite not feeling well after returning to Pochow, G. P. continued visiting outstations. One Sunday during such a visit, Lena, his wife, took his temperature and found that it was over 102 degrees. She and Wade took him to Attie's house in Kweiteh, where he stayed until being taken to the hospital on the following Tuesday. Doctors prayed for him and provided medical attention. Other Chinese Christians also prayed for him. An elderly colporteur told G. P. that he had done so much good work and had so much merit that God would heal him, to which G. P. responded, "I have *no* merit."[45]

During the early stages of his illness G. P. retained a sense of humor. On his second day in the hospital, he got out of bed to get something but fell to the floor. Attie, who had stepped out of the room with Lena, ran back to the room and said, "'Why Pleasant you should not try to get up. Did you fall hard?' And even then his wit came out. 'No, I fell easy, but I can't get up easy!'"[46]

---

[44] Attie Bostick to G. P. Bostick's Children: Adelaide, Bertha, Mattie, Sam, and Thornton, June 22, 1926.
[45] Ibid.
[46] Ibid.

G. P., however, became delusional during his last days, "holding meetings, appointing committees, etc. [in his mind]. He sang part of a Chinese hymn, 'Spirit Divine, Attend Our Prayers' and also prayed in Chinese. Every time anyone asked him how he was, he answered in his cheerful way, 'Better, thank you.' He was so patient and so easy to wait on—not a word of complaint at anytime, and even at five yesterday morning he swallowed a little milk and Benger's food, by my just putting the spoon to his mouth. I was so glad they brought him here and to my place first, and as I kept trying to do different things to be all the help I could, I recalled his faithful service he gave me 22 years ago when I had Typhoid on our way, moving to Pochow."[47]

Following G. P.'s death, Christians in Kweiteh held a funeral service for G. P. in the hospital chapel, and three Chinese Christians "spoke most tearfully and gratefully of his long, useful years here, and of how appropriate it was that he should go to his heavenly home from here, referring to how he endured hardships years ago to come all the way from Taian down here to preach and encourage the interested ones. Pastor Dong read the first chapter of Philippians and 2 Tim. 4:6-8. We sang the old hymn he loved so much, 'There is a fountain filled with blood and at the grave, / Safe in The Arms of Jesus,' in Chinese, and there were two prayers."[48]

Attie encouraged G. P.'s children to read Psalm 46, which he had included in a telegraph to his children after his second wife's death in 1903 and which Attie had found him reading fourteen days later. "Read it again," Attie suggested, and go to God "for comfort in this sad hour. He is the only *source of true comfort for all time.*"[49]

Attie closed the letter by reminding the children of their father's love for them: "You have a precious memory. He loved you and was interested in all you were interested in, and prayed and longed for your best in Christ. He is the only one who can keep [you] in the last trying hour. May He bless your all and help you to love and serve him."[50]

In September 1926 Attie moved to Pochow to assist her brother Wade, Flora, and the remaining missionaries there. In November, Attie accompanied her sister-in-law Lena to Shanghai. Having served as a Southern Baptist mis-

---

[47] Ibid.
[48] Ibid.
[49] Ibid.
[50] Ibid.

sionary in Pochow for almost fourteen years, Lena Bostick boarded a steamer and returned home to Virginia.[51]

Continued Political Unrest, 1927-1928

Attie was in charge of the evangelistic work in Pochow, which included evening prayer meetings and teacher's meetings. Several groups of Chinese Christians (some of which were accompanied by Attie and Grace Stribling, the superintendent of the mission's day school) traveled to nearby villages, "singing and preaching on the threshing floors and in the court yards."[52] In April 1927 the missionaries had to flee Pochow because of civil unrest in the area. Attie worked in Tsingtao (now Qindao), Shantung Province, before going to Shanghai to care for Phil and Mattie White's new baby, who was ill. In September Attie traveled to Tsinan, also in Shantung, to visit in homes and assist with the street chapel until it was safe for her to return to Pochow.[53]

Attie and another missionary, Olive Riddell, returned to Pochow on March 20, 1928. Attie described the scene:

> though our property was all occupied by soldiers, the Christians had procured for our use part of the large egg-plant building, within a few yards of my brother Wade's home. It was a joy to greet these brethren and sisters in the Lord again and to find out how well they had all been cared for by our kind Father while we had been away for eleven months. Most of them had remained faithful, and they had not forgotten to pray for us while we were away, and many expressed how they felt as orphans because we were away, and that they felt there was still a large and necessary place for their missionary friends to fill.[54]

Soldiers had smashed or sold most of the missionaries' jars of cherries; torn up several rose bushes and trees; and stolen a mattress, a bed, a kitchen table, and Flora's dishes. The situation undoubtedly could have been worse, but "the servants were very faithful in looking after things."[55]

About a month after arriving back in Pochow, Attie and Riddell began holding worship services in the city chapel. Attie resumed visiting women and leading prayer meetings. She also quizzed women and children on how well they had learned their gospel lessons. Attie noted the wonderful opportunity

---

[51] Attie Bostick to Judie Bostick, November 13, 1926. Although still listed in the Southern Baptist *Annual* for 1928, 1929, and 1930 as serving in Kweiteh, Attie worked in Pochow from September 1926 to May 1929. See Attie's service record in the League, Attie T. Bostick folder, FMBCC, Box 33, SBHLA.
[52] *Annual*, SBC, 1928, 188.
[53] Ibid.
[54] *Annual*, SBC, 1929, 205.
[55] Attie Bostick to Bertha Bostick, May 7, 1928.

she had in sharing the gospel with "boys and girls in the city. They do not have school on Sundays, and may come to our services."⁵⁶

Because the situation remained dangerous, Riddell decided not to open the mission school and not to travel to the country outstations. Instead, she and Attie started a Bible class for women who could read. Later in the fall, when the conditions improved, Riddell and a group of Chinese Christians visited nine outstations, holding evangelistic meetings in fifty-two villages near the stations. "There were large crowds everywhere we went," she observed. "People not only seemed willing but eager to hear."⁵⁷

"Olive Riddell"- Attie Bostick. "Taken in Shanghai, Jan. 29, 1931" (unknown)

Wade also returned to Pochow in 1928, but his wife and their daughter, Oreon, had returned to America in August to enroll Oreon in college and to assist Wade, Jr., who was a college student.⁵⁸ Wade described the tense situation when he arrived back in Pochow. All of the missionaries' homes were occupied by soldiers, though they vacated two houses three days later. One day, "a large number of soldiers passed immediately through our field in pursuit of the retreating Northern Army. We met the leader of the Southern forces and found him friendly and helpful, but so decidedly Southern that he asked us plainly if we were Imperialists and whether or not we favored the new form of government. From his question we saw that we needed to be most careful both as to our talking and acting."⁵⁹

While the missionaries had been gone from Pochow, Wade noted:

> Much had been done to poison the minds of the people and we did not know how deeply rooted these anti-foreign, anti-Christian ideas were in their minds. To our delight we were received as old friends, and neigh-

---

⁵⁶ *Annual*, SBC, 1929, 205.
⁵⁷ Ibid.
⁵⁸ Ibid.
⁵⁹ Ibid., 206.

bors—their interest shown in us being marked and unmistakable. As to our church members, we would but praise the Lord, that there was scarcely any turning away. One Chinese brother, with tears in his eyes, rejoiced with me in this steadfastness of the brethren. This time of testing has of course had its desired effect upon the church in the deepening of the religious experiences of some and the falling away of a few. Two of the most loved and appreciated brethren have died during the year largely, if not wholly, as the result of the hard times. They were most fine characters and had been closely associated with us for a long time.[60]

The Work in Pochow, 1929

During 1929 the mission work in Pochow began to return to normal. Riddell and Greene Strother, another Pochow missionary, directed the work at the Pochow outstations. Despite the presence of soldiers, in the spring and the fall, Pastor Tung and Riddell traveled to all nine outstations and other villages where Christians lived. Riddell held classes for women, and in the summer, she held a class for women who could read.[61]

Strother, who was sent to Pochow "to take up the work of the late lamented G. P. Bostick," and several Chinese preachers and colporteurs led an eight-week evangelistic campaign aimed "at preaching the gospel in every village of a large section of the southeast. In this campaign there were 229 professions of faith, 550 villages reached, 12,000 Gospel portions sold." Despite the success of the campaign outside of Pochow, "thousands of soldiers, hostile to our work, ruined our proposed campaign" in the city. Bandits also hindered missionary work.[62]

Attie's Furlough

The years 1922 to 1929 were difficult for Attie. She had suffered the loss of her older brother G. P., and Wade's family had returned to the states. The end of her seven years of service qualifying her for a furlough had arrived in 1929, and this time, Attie was ready return to North Carolina and spend time with her many nieces and nephews and her beloved sister Judie.[63] She sailed for America on April 6, 1929.

---

[60] Ibid.
[61] *Annual*, SBC, 1930, 197.
[62] *Annual*, SBC, 1930, 197.
[63] On October 10, 1927, Judie married J.D. Eskridge. He died on April 26, 1935.

Chapter Five

ATTIE'S "PATCH WORK"
1930-1938

> Bless the LORD, O my soul: and all that is within me,
> bless his holy name. (Ps. 103:1)

Attie's Return to a War-Torn Country

After a well-deserved furlough, Attie left again for China on January 7, 1931, returning to the mission station in Kweiteh, where she resumed working with Sarah and Sidney Townshend. While Attie was in America during 1930, the Townshends had a terrifying year. Japanese soldiers occupied their mission compound from January until August, and in March the Townshends' home was looted three times and their lives were threatened by "ruffians who demanded money and heroin." All the rooms in their house were shot into and the church building was badly damaged. Fortunately, no one was harmed, including the Chinese Christians, whose homes were shelled. Although the Townshends were unable to leave their compound to do their country work early in the year, Chinese evangelists visited 251 villages in the spring.[1]

After she had been back in China for several months, Attie reported to the Foreign Mission Board (FMB) that in July 1931 she and a Chinese woman traveled to Hsuchow to visit Christians and others who were interested in hearing the gospel. Attie had helped her brother G. P. organize a church in that city in 1926. She noted, "I was much encouraged in this visit, as I always am in my visits to the country Christians. There is a warm-hearted interest there." The purchase of a Ford automobile enabled her and the Townshends to travel more easily to the outstations, for which she was grateful: "There are many things to encourage and there are many of the opposite nature, but I am thankful, very thankful, I was permitted to come back and take up the work again. I am the most thankful for Jesus Christ, the same yesterday, today and forever. Pray for us and for your brethren and sisters among the Chinese."[2]

In November, Attie wrote to her family back home, and along with the letter she sent her niece Bertha some money to employ a cook. Attie told Bertha not to worry

---

[1] *Annual*, Southern Baptist Convention (SBC), 1931, 210.
[2] *Annual*, SBC, 1932, 203.

about receiving the money because "God has been good in supplying my every need and so I can help you this time and not miss it." Attie also described a meeting held at the Kweiteh mission, to which 125 people ("a lot of dear old women") had come from the outstations, some walking thirty miles. The mission held prayer services at seven a.m. each morning, two worship services during the day, and one at night. Attie played records of Chinese singing hymns at the beginning of the services. "Not all who came were church members," Attie noted, "but many were enquirers and a number were examined and passed for baptism, to take that step next fall, and if they prove faithful up to that time." Those interested in becoming Christians included four men. At the Sunday morning service, six women were baptized, and eighty-eight celebrated the Lord's Supper. Despite having a "raspy throat" and not being able to sing or talk, Attie had attended all the services.[3]

In a letter written on December 15, 1931, to her sister-in-law Lena Bostick, Attie described such mundane things as Christmas presents and her efforts to furnish and decorate her home in Kweiteh, but she also mentioned the death of her brother John, who was twenty-two years older than she. "Yes, there is a sadness that dear John has left us," Attie wrote to Lena, "but also thankfulness that he did not have a long, lingering illness, and he was VERY LONELY after Betty's [his wife's] death. I felt I was saying a last good-bye when we parted last January and he did too. He sobbed and showed his feelings more than I ever saw him. He was always so brave about that. He wrote me very faithfully too, but I think my last letter did not reach him."[4]

Also in her letter, Attie expressed her sorrow at learning that Lena and her sisters had suffered a financial disaster because of a bank failure, a reference to the Great Depression that was in its early stages in the United States. Attie's finances, however, remained stable, and she assured her sister-in-law that she had been "spared" financial ruin, for which she was "very thankful." Attie described for Lena how much she, her brother Wade, and the Townshends paid for cooks; how much certain food items cost; and how much she paid for dental work. Attie also noted that she gave one month's salary to the FMB for its debt, a month's salary to Judson College, and "$50.00 to Boiling Springs." Despite her living expenses and charity, she noted proudly that she was still able to donate money for flood relief in China and for Bibles for people who needed them.[5]

---

[3] Attie Bostick to Loved Ones, November 21, 1931.
[4] Attie Bostick to Lena Bostick, December 15, 1931. See also Attie Bostick to Bertha Bostick, December 16, 1931.
[5] Attie Bostick to Lena Bostick, December 15, 1931.

The 1932 Famine

During 1932 another famine struck China. The streets of Kweiteh and the surrounding country towns were soon piled high with furniture, household goods, and farm tools as residents sold their possessions to purchase food. In order to help provide employment to assist the Chinese, the Kweiteh missionaries hired fifty coolies to work on the roads in the suburbs and an additional 350 to build roads. "We do not believe in direct relief," Sidney Townshend informed the FMB, "but this relief arrived so late in the spring that there was no other way to get it to the poor people in time. Several thousand dollars were distributed in this way."[6]

The famine did not hinder the spiritual ministry of the Kweiteh missionaries. Townshend preached to the coolies on Sundays, and at Che Ch'eng Hsien, a nearby country town, land was purchased and a chapel was built using local funding for two-thirds of the cost. At U Hong K'eo, the first outstation at which a chapel had been built in 1916, the original building was demolished and a new one was constructed, even though bandits had harassed the construction workers. The women's work also increased and the Woman's Missionary Union contributed "a quite nice sum towards the work of pioneering." When Pastor Fan of Kaifeng preached at some meetings in the fall, the Kweiteh station had the largest attendance of outsta-

"At our Thanksgiving dinner. Mrs. Rome, Mrs. Strother, Miriam on Mrs. Townshend's lap, Miss Riddell, Flora, Miss Dawes—Bottom. Mr. Avent Strother, Hans Wolfe, Townshend, I (in Adelaide's Dress), Stantons…Please send to Berfy & let her see my *new* dress! Mr. Rome snapped this & Patt & Victor Lee were asleep."—Attie Bostick c. Nov. 1932

---

[6] *Annual*, SBC, 1933, 187.

tion members in many years. Twelve people were baptized, and six others were accepted for baptism at a later date.[7]

Attie's Care of Her Sister-in-Law Flora Bostick

Amid the famine relief and other work in Kweiteh, Attie was once again called on to care for physical needs of a fellow missionary. Her sister-in-law Flora had contracted tuberculosis in 1931, and after nine months of little improvement, she went with her husband, Wade, to the mountains, where her condition improved initially.[8] In August 1932 Attie traveled to the mountain town of Kuling (now Lushan), Jiangxi Province, to stay with Flora so that Wade could return to his work in Pochow.

During her trip to Kuling, which was 300 miles south of Kweiteh, Attie spent a day and a half on a steamer, before being carried in a wicker chair by six bearers to her destination. In a letter to her niece Adelaide, Attie revealed how accustomed she had become to living in China: "I had a deck cabin, to myself and plenty of room and I was bold enough to leave my door and two windows open at night. I was the only English speaking person on there and felt just as at home as among my own people in Shelby."[9]

Upon arriving in Kuling, Attie provided loving attention to Flora's physical needs:

> I helped her get a tub bath and the next few days after she had quite a bit of blood in her sputum. She moans a lot in her sleep and doesn't get refreshing sleep. You see she had pleurisy at 16 years of age and her right lung has been weak ever since then. She has forced herself to eat and take four yard eggs a day, but has held up on that the past few days—just turned against things. I've rubbed her a good deal with Vicks. That helps her some. She is on a porch all the time. It is a plank house, built by some California man, very compact and very convenient. She likes ice cream and I'm going to see if we can't have it twice a day for her. It will have eggs and milk, both of which will be good for her.[10]

Attie's Return to the Pochow Station

After caring for Flora in August, Attie returned to Kweiteh for a month. In October 1932 she transferred to Pochow because Wade had returned to Kuling to care for his terminally ill wife. Back in Pochow, Attie resumed her evangelistic work. She and others spent January 1, 1933, "in fasting and prayer for a world wide revival."

---

[7] Ibid.
[8] Ibid., 187-88.
[9] Attie Bostick (Pao Au Deh) to Adelaide Bostick (Lao Peng Yu), August 5, 1932. In this letter Attie used their Chinese names. See also Attie Bostick to Friend at Judson College, Marion, Alabama, August 20, 1932.
[10] Attie Bostick (Pao Au Deh) to Adelaide Bostick (Lao Peng Yu), August 5, 1932

Children's programs at the Pochow mission during the year bore fruit, as some children became Christians and others memorized scripture. At the beginning of the year, Attie had promised to give "a sixty cent Bible" to everyone who memorized the "Golden texts." She presented thirty-four Bibles to people whose ages ranged from seven to fifty-five.[11]

Other programs during 1933 also proved to be successful. "Fifty have followed Christ in baptism this year," Attie reported to the FMB. "Our Saturday night prayer meeting has been a great spiritual blessing to all who have attended, and the attendance increases. The women meet on Wednesday for Bible study and prayer; and a general evangelistic meeting is held on Wednesday evenings."[12]

Attie's "Patch Work"

Despite the change of climate to the cooler mountains of Kuling, Flora never recovered from her illness. The 1935 Southern Baptist *Annual* included Wade's report about his wife's death: "The first hundred days of this year [1934] were the completion of Mrs. Bostick's eleven hundred days of an unprecedented, but

"At our Jan. Bible Class."—Attie Bostick c. 1934 (Attie is at the far left; Wade is in the middle with hat.)

---

[11] *Annual*, SBC, 1934, 202.
[12] Ibid.

"Tsao Fu Tien & wife—just after they married 6 o'clock a.m. Time exposure. For Lena."—Attie Bostick c. 1934

losing struggle against a serious complication of pellagra and other maladies, resulting in her home going."[13] After burying his wife in Kuling, Wade returned to Pochow, where he and Attie continued their mission work.

Attie described her "work, as much of my life," as "patch work, visiting in the homes with Mrs. Wen, the Bible woman, whose faith and perseverance have inspired faith in me; and meeting weekly with the women in study of God's word, and prayer meetings at our church Wednesday, Saturday and Sunday nights." Attie hosted a class in her home in 1934, during which students read the New Testament, John Bunyan's *Pilgrim's Progress*, and "the life of a very earnest Christian in China." Also, one thirteen-year-old girl memorized 365 Bible verses, despite not being "allowed to attend any of our meetings regularly, and her folks do not believe. She rightly earned a Bible, and she tells me she reads it every day and prays."[14]

The Pochow mission station covered an area of 3,600 square miles, with a total population of over two million people. Within that area there were more than 18,000 towns and villages, and three major cities: Pochow with 150,000 people, Yung Cheng with 30,000, and Lui with 15,000. Seven churches with

---

[13] *Annual*, SBC, 1935, 183.
[14] Ibid.

530 members existed in the area. Attie was in charge of the North River Church in Pochow. Nineteen men and four women Chinese workers assisted the ministry of the six Southern Baptist missionaries: Attie, Miss Clifford Barratt, Harriett King, Mary King, and Greene and Martha Strother. The work for 1935 included holding revival meetings, instructing candidates for baptism, and teaching the Bible in several churches. Although muddy roads made travel difficult, many Chinese attended these meetings. Some women who still had bound feet walked as many as fifty miles to hear the gospel message.[15]

"At our dining table with my back to our sitting room, the sliding doors open between—I look 'scared'!! Taken Dec. 1934."—Attie Bostick

In a March 1935 letter to someone identified only as Ural, Attie described some of her "patch work," which was often difficult and dangerous:

> Saturday, Wade and I started out in the Ford, just after our breakfast and morning prayers, and visited four of our outstations and got back in time for me to teach my Sunday School Class at church here [Pochow] yesterday morning and then attend church. We had meant to have the noon service at still another place and visit several more in the p.m., but the first thunderstorm of the season came up about three o'clock Sunday morning, and after breakfast the rain began peppering down, so we came back home—the forty miles we had gone. We had driven through dust so deep a time or two the car skidded, so we knew it would be no joke to try driving through that after a heavy rain. The roads do fairly well when it is dry, but we just do not try to use the Ford after it rains hard. Wade had heard also that bandits were near where we were spending the night, even carrying off hostages from the city we were in and he felt we should not delay and maybe tempt them to try to get us.[16]

---

[15] *Annual*, SBC, 1936, 183. According to Wayne Flynt and Gerald W. Berkley, some Chinese women had their feet bound at an early age because "tiny feet emphasized a woman's aristocratic status and indicated that she did not perform the chores common among lower-class women." Wayne Flynt and Gerald W. Berkley, *Taking Christianity to China: Alabama Missionaries in the Middle Kingdom, 1850-1950* (Tuscaloosa: The University of Alabama Press, 1997), 194. See also Catherine B. Allen, *The New Lottie Moon Story* (Nashville: Broadman Press, 1980).
[16] Attie Bostick to Ural [?], March 18, 1935.

Attie also described for Ural some of the worship services and classes she and Wade had attended at some of the outstations:

> We stopped at two outstations where meetings had been on for five days. At the first they were divided off into classes, all studying the Bible or some portion. The evangelist's wife was teaching a short prayer to the very beginners, so we did not tarry long there as each one felt they must greet us separately, and of course that greatly interfered with their class work. The next place we reached just as they were starting the twelve o'clock, or noon service, so we stayed and heard our evangelist preach on Zacchaeus' conversion, stressing how he gave his all to the Lord. Then he [the evangelist] asked for names of the ones who would promise a tenth to the Lord, and some 5 promised, and there were only seven church members present I think. The others are enquirers. At all the places the women are more than men. . . . We went to still another place and ate our lunch we had carried along, saw the evangelist and his family, heard the daughter who was recently baptized repeat the Bible verses she had learned while up here, had a rest and from there went to a City where we have had a church place over twenty years. There we spent the night, but I got to visit some dear old sisters who are warm hearted and have learned to read the Bible since they became interested. That night we had a meeting at our chapel and Wade talked to them on Peter's deliverance from prison, which was the Sunday School lesson for the next day. We had only covered 40 miles, but saw a lot of our work.[17]

These excursions with her brother to the outstations soon ended, for in 1935 Wade returned to the United States. For the first time since 1900, Attie would work in China without one of her brothers being nearby.

Attie's 1936 Correspondence with Charles Maddry

On January 21, 1936, Attie wrote Charles Maddry and his wife of her concern about the new modernist theology and the Southern Baptists' proposal to build a large seminary in Shanghai. In 1933 Maddry became the FMB's corresponding secretary, succeeding T. Bronson Ray, who served in that capacity from 1928 to 1932.

As in previous letters to other corresponding secretaries, Attie did not shy away from expressing her opinions to Maddry. Attie informed the corresponding secretary about a sermon titled "About the Bible," which she had heard Gordon Poteat preach in Shanghai. She wished that Maddry could have heard the sermon while he had been in the city, for "I feel you would consider more seriously the opinion

---

[17] Ibid. See also Wade Bostick to Homefolks, March 19, 1935, in the Bostick, Wade D. folder, Foreign Mission Board Correspondence Collection, Box 8, Southern Baptist Historical Library and Archives, Nashville, TN.

of the MAJORITY of Southern Baptists as to our connection with an institution that preaches such modernism."[18] Attie chose not to hear Poteat's subsequent sermons on miracles and on the resurrection.[19]

Another issue that rankled Attie was the Southern Baptists Convention's (SBC) plan "to make a BIG SEMINARY in Shanghai," which she considered to "be a grievous mistake. Unless a great change has come over our people in the South, the ones who give to Foreign Missions do not favor such modernism as Gordon Poteat preached last summer in saying we need not accept all the Bible and rejecting part did not mean the rejecting all." Attie hoped that the SBC would "sever connections with such an institution if it means the giving to the Northern Baptists or the Chinese all that Southern Baptists have put in there. I believe you will be blessed of God in taking such a step, and I feel it will be a drag for us so long as we go on trying to keep up relations with that unorthodox institution."[20]

Attie also addressed a topic that had bothered her for many years—the FMB's debt. When Maddry became the corresponding secretary in 1933, the debt had grown to over $1 million.[21] She assured Maddry that if she "were able I would, without delay, wipe out our disgrace—that debt. I am so thankful it is getting less. It should never have been made. 'Owe no man anything except to love him' [Rom. 13:8]." To that end, Attie sent Mrs. Maddry a sweater and some cross-stitch to sell "and so add a little more to lessen the debt."[22]

In a postscript to the letter, Attie referred to some medical problems she had had. In 1935 she had a cancerous growth on her nose, which was treated with radium. She received her last treatment on October 9, 1935, and she reported to the Maddrys that "there has been no trouble since. Psalms 103:1-3."[23]

---

[18] Modernism was another term for "liberalism." See H. W. Pipin, "Liberalism, Baptist Views," in *Dictionary of Baptists in America*, ed. Bill J. Leonard (Downers Grove, IL: InterVarsity Press, 1994), 172-73, and Wayne E. Ward and W. Boyd Hunt, "Liberalism," in *Encyclopedia of Southern Baptists* (Nashville: Broadman Press, 1958), 2:785-86.
[19] Attie Bostick to Charles and Mrs. Maddry, January 21, 1936.
[20] Ibid.
[21] Under Maddry's leadership, Southern Baptists eliminated the debt in 1943, making the FMB debt free for the first time since its inception in 1845. See Baker J. Cuthen, "Maddry, Charles Edward," in *Encyclopedia of Southern Baptists* (Nashville: Broadman Press, 1971), 3:1818.
[22] Attie to Charles and Mrs. Maddry, January 21, 1936.
[23] Ibid.

In a subsequent letter to Maddry, Attie again addressed the FMB's debt and her own attempts at reducing it:

> I enclose a letter of credit for my October salary, which please place on payment of the Foreign Mission Debt. I am sorry it is already delayed. I held it hoping to have time to write you how I have enjoyed getting out in the country work this autumn, in a way that you might use it to encourage others to hasten the wiping out this disgrace on our FMB. . . . Since 1919, I have yearly given one month's salary toward debt, besides the dollar per month the past two years, and one or two years I was able to give two months' salary. I just wish I might give enough at one sweep to wipe it all out.[24]

Attie also noted the work of Harriette King and Martha Strother, two of her fellow missionaries, and how they all contributed money from their own salaries to help support Lois Prosser, an independent missionary who taught phonetics in Pochow. They were happy to provide for this woman, but such support, Attie vented to Maddry, would not be necessary "if only our brethren and sisters over there [in America] will wipe out that debt, and obey Him in giving the Gospel to the lost, then we will join you in praise and thanksgiving."[25]

Attie's Anxious Moments

After returning to North Carolina, Wade developed a serious health problem that required surgery. Judie wrote Attie about the upcoming surgery, but Attie then had to wait two tense weeks to hear of the results. She expressed her anxiety in a letter to Wade on May 3, 1936:

> Yesterday ended the longest two weeks time I ever passed in China, bringing word from Judie that you had had your operation and were recovering. Her card, saying you had gone to the Hospital for a major operation, had reached me April the 18th. Fortunately, they were very busy weeks, but I studied carefully the arrival of foreign mail in Shanghai, and then waited eagerly for the arrival here till yesterday's brought me her letter. . . . Anyway we are very thankful to know you came through the operation successfully, and trust you will soon be stronger than formerly.[26]

Attie ended the letter with these words: "Love to you and my new sister."[27] Attie's "new sister" was Estelle Perry Gough. Upon his return to North Carolina, Wade fell in love with Estelle, whom he married on March 26, 1936.

---

[24] Attie Bostick to Charles Maddry, November 28, 1936.
[25] Ibid.
[26] Pien Shang Shin and Hsu Chi Chang to Wade Bostick, May 3, 1936. Pien Shang Shin and Hsu Chi Chang were former students of Wade. Attie's letter is contained in their letter.
[27] Ibid.

Attie Bostick and Bible Class, c. 1936

Attie's Ministry in 1936

From December 31, 1935 to January 14, 1936, the Pochow station held several special meetings, which Attie described in a report to the FMB. Seventy people, fifty-five men and fifteen women, attended the meetings. More women did not attend because the meetings were held during "the busiest time of the whole year for Chinese women," and because "it is not easy for them, walking twenty miles and put their quilt on their backs (for cover as they sleep on wheat straw) and trudge in, but some of them did this!!"[28]

Students assembled every morning before breakfast to pray, memorize Bible verses, and hear devotional messages. After breakfast, the students attended a Bible study taught by a Chinese minister. Attie enjoyed these Bible studies, and the students' love for the Bible pleased her: "My heart thrilled with joy" as the teacher "asked those who believed with sincerity EVERY WORD of the Bible, to hold up their hands, and EVERY hand went up." Attie then contrasted the students' attitude toward the Bible with that of Gordon Poteat's:

> (I sincerely wished the Professor I had listened to from Shanghai University last summer in Shanghai, when he so ruthlessly explained we need not believe all the Bible, and our rejecting some portions, did not mean we must reject all, might have seen that class of simple believers—but not "simpletons" by any means. Then we read prophecies of the Old Testament and their fulfillment to a word concerning Israel, and then of Christ and their fulfillment in the New.) Our hearts 'burned within us' as one lesson after another showed God's plan fulfilled. Really, I rejoiced in this class study as I never had in Bible Study in our English language.[29]

After the morning Bible study, the students sang for several hours before attending a Bible study on the Jesus' commandments, taught by Greene Strother. Several class members had memorized the Sermon on the Mount and "were asked to stand up and explain the meaning of different portions, and they showed they had given study to the scripture." After students rested from one to two o'clock, Miss Clifford Irene Barratt taught a Bible class, using the Chinese Bible. At night students attended another study on Jesus' commandments. These students spent a total of six hours each day in Bible study.[30]

By 1936 the Pochow station was serving approximately 20,000 villages, with only one foreign missionary pastor, Greene Strother; twenty Chinese

---

[28] Attie Bostick, "Report to the Foreign Mission Board: The Bible Class-Pochow, Dec. 31-Jan 14, 1935-1936," c. 1936, in the League, Attie T. Bostick folder, Foreign Mission Board Correspondence Collection (FMBCC), Box 33, Southern Baptist Historical Library and Archives (SBHLA), Nashville, TN.
[29] Ibid. See Luke 24:32 for the reference to their hearts "burning within us."
[30] Ibid.

evangelists; six Bible women; and four women missionaries: Attie, Martha Strother, Harriett King, and Harriett's mother, Dr. Mary L. King, who was on furlough in 1936.

Attie felt "privileged" to accompany Greene Strother "on his rounds, holding meetings at eight places" during the fall of 1936.[31] Chinese Christians had been studying "the catechism, duties of church members, and Believers creed," whenever time permitted.[32] The dedication of the Chinese Christians filled her heart with "gratitude and praise to the Lord of the harvest for the great interest manifested everywhere. Many of the women who attended the month's Bible class in the spring are going with the [revival] tent or in groups telling of Jesus. Some of them have not one quilt to cover with these nights when the ice is half an inch thick. At one place straw, for the women to sleep on, had been spread over the whole room and as I went to my cot one night I had to walk carefully not to tread on those already asleep." Several women were ill, "and two were troubled with demon possession." One woman had to leave a meeting because her infant kept crying, so she asked Attie to teach her "'NOW.' In the darkness of the late night when all should have been asleep this woman was taught the text, 'Create in me a clean heart O Lord, and renew a right Spirit within me' [Ps. 51:10]."[33] Attie's heart ached, however, as she thought of the many women who wanted to know more of the gospel. She recalled another young mother who, in order to attend some meetings, "had left a year-old, nursing baby at home . . . —the first time she had ever been to such. And she contributed some for the repairing of the old straw covered house too while there."[34] Even after more than thirty years in China, Attie was still amazed by how many people wanted to learn about the Bible and how many gladly made financial sacrifices to further the gospel message.

---

[31] *Annual*, SBC, 1937, 224.
[32] Attie Bostick to Friends in Christ, October 10, 1936.
[33] *Annual*, SBC, 1937, 225.
[34] Attie Bostick to Charles Maddry, November 28, 1936.

Attie's Ministry for 1937

Attie began 1937 by working in a two-week Bible class held in Pochow. Afterward she and a Chinese woman visited women who had shown an interest in the gospel, encouraging "them to persevere in coming to our services and studying our regular course for the women."[35]

During these days Attie filled her diary with the fruits of many years of work among the Chinese, with accounts of her ministry, with mundane events, and with happy and tragic events.[36] She spent her happiest times visiting the Chinese in their villages, where many were willing to hear and receive the gospel. Following are the entries from her diary for January through April 1937:

"Love to dear Judie-Attie, May 1937"

- Jan. 1, 1937—"Bless the Lord O my soul and all that is within me bless His holy name."

We met from eight a.m. to one p.m. in prayer for a worldwide revival today. Only nine to begin with but fifteen later. Pastor Strother then Mrs. Strother, and I the last hour. The Lord was there. I had felt specially burdened to pray for our Christians to keep our Lord's Day holy. The young neighbor who led, prayed and acknowledged he did not, asked God to help him do it. I praise God for the privilege of prayer. "He is able."

Mrs. Strother and I visited a widow with a five days old baby girl. They with the other four children, on a pallet, on the ground, under the gateway, while the coffin with her dead husband's body occupied their only living room (died October 14th, awaiting the magistrate's decision as to a law-suit. He committed suicide).

---

[35] Attie Bostick to Charles Maddry, April, 5, 1937.
[36] Attie Bostick's diary, in the League, Attie T. Bostick folder, FMBCC, Box 33, SBHLA.

• Jan. 5. With Pastor Strother's help finally got my treasurer's report off to Shanghai. At four went to see an old blind sister (widow) whose face was badly swollen and covered with blisters. Says she prays all the time to her Lord to take her to Himself.

• Jan. 11. Met at Pastor Strother's, and had a good, profitable day in consultation and prayer. Made our budget and prayer list for this year.

• 15-Took Sheo Lan her little booklet for learning a verse a day from the Bible. Am VERY tired tonight.

• 22-Wade's birthday and the Strothers ate with me. Word comes that Dr. Harris had been operated on for appendicitis. I am thankful for the good brother whose birthday it is.

• Feb. 2-Bible Class on and three meetings a day keep me busy, with trying to be organist and dispense eye and other medicines as the different ones need. My Gardener's brother just home from Kweiteh Hospital, where I kept him over a month—worse than when he went. They think he cannot live long.

• Feb. 10-Chinese New Year and some visitors—mostly just the very curious ones. We are having special meetings at our church.

• 25-Mrs. Wen and I had very encouraging visits in a courtyard where the enquirers repeated the Six Salvation Plan Tracts (Bible Verses).

• Mar. 8-Special meetings for training some men and boys for special evangelistic preaching in the unreached villages. Some forty going, two together to witness in each village.

• 11-Went with Pastor Strother in the Ford and we joined one party, witnessing in eight villages.

• 9-Joined another band and made nine villages, witnessing, selling Bible Portions, and singing choruses. I love to hold the Scripture Portion open at the picture while others preach.

- 16-Not a victorious day, considering self too much.

- 17-Lost considerable time trying to find one of the [Evangelistic] Bands, so went to our forty mile distant Chapel hoping to get a deed to Chapel registered, but failed.

- Sat. Mar. 20. God gave me The Trial and Crucifixion of our Lord as subject for our English (missionary) prayer – meeting.

- 23. Out to our West field for the village preaching and SO thankful for the interest shown, and the Scripture Portions sold. So many School children buy these. It is THY word, Father, and Thou hast promised it shall not return unto Thee void.

- Mar. 30. Most of the day on my treasurer's report – went twice to Strothers about it and once to the City (a mile away). It is still unfinished, but doesn't lack much. I do want to honor Him in all my ways and be pleasing to Him.

- April 1. To the forty mile Chapel again to try and register the deed. Magistrate just been changed. Nothing doing!

- 2. It was a pleasure hearing two little six year olds singing choruses, one the son of an evangelist and one the daughter of a former school boy and whose mother taught in Miss Riddell's School. Caught up with an evangelistic band and went with them to four new villages—sold 200 Portions.

- 7-Got off early for the South Country where new work has just begun –one village has no idols in it, all claim to believe. They have learned to sing quite a few hymns. "Jesus Shall Reign Where're the Sun," etc., they learned by heart but knew no tune! We tried to sing it with them. This is my most encouraging visit of all these 37 years in His work in China.

- 25-Forty-one baptized. Two hundred and fourteen partook of our Lord's Supper. This ended our Spring Big Meeting, at which Pastor Chao did very faithful preaching of His word.

- 26-Began paying salaries at 5:45 a.m. and been at it most of the day.

- 29-Visited in nine homes. Heard Sheo Lan say Matt. 6, John 14, Acts 12, 2, 5, Eph. 3, 1 Tim. 4. How I praise Him and she loves His word thus, and can "hide it upon her heart."

- May 10-Mrs. Ch'en who worked for Flora 20 yrs. ago, called to tell me she is a Christian, tho' she paid no attention to Flora's tearful pleadings in those days.

In a letter to Charles Maddry in April, Attie mentioned that she was scheduled for a furlough in 1938 and that she desired "to return" to China in 1939 "and continue in His work so long as my health permits. When I was coming out from Gastonia First Church in 1900, I expressed the wish before Deacon J. D. Moore of sainted memory, that I hoped the Lord would spare me to be an old woman in His work in China, and he said he felt the Lord would grant that wish." Although she was nearly sixty-two years old, Attie emphasized: "I do not YET consider myself an old woman!"[37]

Attie also informed Maddry that she had made five trips to the villages where the people had never heard the gospel. When she could ride in Greene Strother's car, she and two Chinese workers visited seven villages a day, and then held a meeting wherever they stopped for the night. Attie described how they gathered worshippers for their night meetings:

> We would stop on a threshing floor, singing "Come to Jesus", and other simple hymns, and then when the crowd had assembled, Jesus was preached to them. They listened with good interest. Only once or twice when sin was preached, did an opposer speak up and say "we are ALL good." I believe many will be among the redeemed at the Last Day because of this witnessing. Scripture portions went rapidly in selling of them. It is hard on the men. Windy and dry weather, and we pay them only enough for the simplest food, but most of them have been at it for a month, and have another three weeks.[38]

"An autumn threshing floor in China."—Attie Bostick, c. 1937

---

[37] Attie Bostick to Charles Maddry, April, 5, 1937. Because so many missionaries had been retiring at age sixty-five, Attie's plans to return to China delighted Maddry. See Charles Maddry to Attie Bostick, May 4, 1937.
[38] Attie Bostick to Charles Maddry, April, 5, 1937.

"The point down from <u>our place</u>. There are six or seven forts like this one, over different parts of the mt. & soldiers on guard all the time."—Attie Bostick, c. 1937

Japan's Invasion of China, 1937

In the summer of 1937, Japan invaded China, attacking the northern areas first. When the invasion occurred, many Baptist missionaries were away from their stations; some were on vacation, while others were teaching summer classes at the outstations. Attie heard about the invasion while in the mountains, during a much needed vacation. Having previously lived through several periods of armed conflict in China, she knew what would happen to the railways and lines of communication, so she quietly packed her bags and left the mountains, returning to Pochow before the government authorities could forbid any movement.

Attie decided to remain in China following the Japanese invasion. Notified twice that she would have to leave the country, she methodically prepared to evacuate. The possibility of leaving China discouraged her at times, but Attie put herself in the hands of God, "who more than fifty years ago laid it upon my heart to obey His call and put my life in His hands for service in this land. He heard and answered my prayer and has extended my service a little longer for which I constantly thank Him."[39]

---

[39] Attie Bostick to Charles Maddry, October 31, 1937. See also Attie Bostick, "Report to the Foreign Mission Board for 1937: Pochow, Anhwei, China," December 15, 1937, in the League, Attie T. Bostick folder, FMBCC, Box 33, SBHLA.

After two failed attempts and despite the danger, in late October, Attie resumed her "country work." The Ford, which had served the missionaries well in previous years, consumed too much expensive gasoline, so she hired a rickshaw driver and set out in his "chariot" for the outstations. The spiritual successes at the outstations countered the depressing news of the invasion. The Chinese pastor Chao baptized twenty-four new Christians and celebrated the Lord's Supper with 114 believers, at two outstations. One elderly woman who only a year ago had been "wild with devil possession . . . was calmly studying the Six Tracts on the Plan of Salvation and her changed manner showed she had partaken of that Salvation." The people's interest in the gospel gladdened Attie's heart. At one worship service, the congregation outside the chapel was as large as the one inside. The worshippers contributed over 200 pounds of flour for the common meal and then slept on straw or mats on the dirt floors. No one complained because they "were happy for the opportunity of this meeting."[40]

Attie's Anticipated Furlough

By the end of 1937 almost seven years had passed since her last furlough, so Attie began to prepare for a return to the United States in 1938. The stress of the war between China and Japan, the orders from the American Consulate to evacuate the country, and the constraints on travel to the countryside to visit the outstations had exhausted her. Attie also missed her family and longed to return to them in the spring of 1938. In December 1937 she confided to Judie that she had begun "to count the months now till time to start on furlough, the last of May or 1st of June, and my anticipations are happy ones!"[41]

Happy thoughts about a sweet reunion with her family in North Carolina soon turned into terror. As Attie prepared for her furlough, she learned that Judie had been involved in a life-threatening accident. In a letter to friends and family, Attie's niece Bertha provided the details of Judie's accident. Judie had been wary of her home's water heater all winter, and in December 1937 it exploded while she was in the kitchen making breakfast. Bertha, who was in the house at the time, heard the explosion and ran to help her aunt. The blast broke Judie's right arm and both of her legs below the knees. Unfortunately, doctors determined that Judie's right leg had to be amputated. Bertha reported, however, that Judie was "holding her own wonderfully well; but she

---

[40] Attie Bostick to Charles Maddry, October 31, 1937. See also Bostick, "Report to the Foreign Mission Board for 1937: Pochow, Anhwei, China." Maddry responded to Attie's letter on December 8, 1937.
[41] Attie Bostick to Judie Bostick Eskridge, December 16, 1937.

has two bad burns on the back of her hips where she lies, that are not healing in spite of all they can do (they have an air cushion under her, which makes her more comfortable); and her heart is beating rather fast. So at her age (75) and in her condition there is no telling what turn she may take at any time. Also, she may not come through the operation. But since she has done so well this far, there is hope that she may pull through."[42]

Judie was expected to remain in the hospital for several months. After that, Bertha did not know what she would do with her aunt. "I would never feel safe to leave Aunt Judie alone," she wrote, "and we'll probably get a good colored woman who can look after the house and wait on Aunt Judie while I have to be out. Until Aunt Attie comes home anyway."[43] Before Judie's tragic accident, Attie had considered a furlough necessary for her own spiritual and physical well being. The accident made her furlough an urgent necessity so that she could care for Judie.

Attie left Pochow on February 9, 1938.[44] She had always left China reluctantly, but she had eagerly anticipated her 1938 furlough. Anyone who worked as hard as Attie had worked under uncomfortable and often dangerous conditions deserved to enjoy her time away from the mission field. Yet Attie had learned in China that life was not always fair, and she had met that unfairness with an indomitable spirit that earned her the admiration of her fellow missionaries. Winnie Bennett Ayers praised Attie in her 1938 report to the FMB that after the Japanese invaded China, Attie "in the same quiet spirit, completely unaware of our admiration for her courage, without thought of danger, . . . has gone about her usual work."[45] Caring for Judie would be an opportunity to help her beloved and faithful sister.

---

[42] Bertha Bostick to Friends and Family, December 19, 1937. See also Edith Limer Ledbetter, "The Finest Missionary of Us All," *Royal Service,* June 1960, 40.
[43] Bertha Bostick to Friends and Family, December 19, 1937.
[44] Attie Bostick to Charles Maddry, March 10, 1938.
[45] *Annual*, SBC, 1938, 230.

Chapter Six

ATTIE'S MINISTRY DURING THE JAPANESE OCCUPATION OF CHINA 1938-1941

Thou wilt keep him in perfect peace, whose mind is stayed on thee: because he trusteth in thee. (Isa. 26:3)

And we know that all things work together for good to them that love God, to them who are the called according to his purpose. (Rom. 8:28)

Attie's Furlough, 1938-1939

On February 23, 1938, Attie sailed for America on the *Empress of Asia*. On board the steamer, she wrote to Charles Maddry, the Foreign Mission Board's (FMB) corresponding secretary, about her concern for her sister Judie's health: "I am very anxious to hear how my sister is and hope word will reach me at Victoria [Canada]. I have had a splendid trip this month and more and nothing but Psalm 103 seems adequate to express my feelings."[1] Attie finally arrived in Shelby, North Carolina, on March 17 and immediately began caring for her beloved sister, who was able to return home from the hospital two weeks later on April 2.[2]

During Attie's furlough, Pochow fell to the Japanese army, an event that Greene Strother described in the 1939 Southern Baptist *Annual*. According to Strother, after several days of siege, Japanese troops stormed the city on May 30, 1938. Miss Clifford Barratt and Harriette King huddled in one part of the mission station with more than 1,000 refugees, while Mary King, the Strothers, and their four children waited in another part of the station with about 600 other refugees. Strother reported:

> It had seemed good to us to come out of the city and center all our work north of the river. Miss Barratt and I kept watch at the gates Monday night, but as the Chinese troops had to evacuate in the night and no shot had been fired against the North Suburb, it seemed wise that we open the gates and let the Japanese know the state of affairs. This we did. The Japanese officials have exerted every effort to secure the protection of our property and camps.[3]

---

[1] Attie Bostick to Charles Maddry, March 10, 1938.
[2] Attie Bostick to Gladys Smythwick, September 15, 1938.
[3] *Annual,* Southern Baptist Convention (SBC), 1939, 245-46.

"Pastor Li and me."—G. P. Bostick (front row), c. 1925

The camps remained open for ten weeks, and the missionaries led morning prayers, Bible classes, and vesper services. "We trust," Strother wrote, "that out of these times many will turn unto God and live. Our hearts are filled with praise to God at every remembrance of how he led and protected us through all these days and weeks."[4] Despite the hardships caused by years of war, the school buildings in Pochow, which had been closed for thirteen years, except when they were occupied by soldiers, were re-opened in 1938 and functioned as Christian schools for the children of Chinese Christians. Unfortunately, the evangelistic work during the year often had to be confined to the city because of bandits, but the missionaries did experience several successes, including the ordination of the first Chinese pastor at Pochow, Rev. Chang K'ai Li. Moreover, the total baptisms for the year numbered 305, which was higher than the missionaries had requested in their prayers.[5]

Another missionary, Harriette King, described the fall of Pochow in a letter to her fellow Baptist missionaries Phil and Mattie White in Kweiteh. Ac-

---
[4] Ibid., 246.
[5] Ibid.

cording to King, the Pochow missionaries had advised the residents to flee to the country, as far away from the main roads as possible. The Japanese bombed the city, but the only explosion that caused much loss of life was dropped on May 24, 1938, striking a wedding procession. By the time the Japanese entered the city, most of the people had already left.[6]

As refugees poured into the Pochow mission station, the missionaries tried to present the gospel to as many of them as they could. King noted that "A few are beginning to show encouraging signs of waking up" from their sin. She also expressed her gratitude to God for protecting the missionaries: "Some of our 'visitors' [Japanese] were troublesome but we met with no discourtesy. We have heard many stories of what happened off the church property but nothing such has come to those within our walls. Not only this, but of the Christians that we hear about nearly every day—not one has suffered injury in the country. The Lord has truly been good to us."[7]

Back home in North Carolina, Attie wrote to friends, briefly describing her trip to Ridgecrest Baptist Assembly, a Southern Baptist summer retreat center east of Asheville, North Carolina. In the letter she also praised God for the safety of her fellow Pochow missionaries: "I do praise a kind Father who kept these dear ones through this hard trial."[8]

Even on her furlough Attie still thought about her mission work in Pochow. With Dr. Mary King's retirement imminent, Attie sought ways to find a physician for Pochow. She wrote to Gladys Smythwick, a physician in Lexington, Kentucky, and a former missionary to China, describing Judie's health and asking Smythwick to consider working in Pochow as a medical missionary.

After "the dreadful accident that befell my only living sister," in which Judie's legs were broken in three places, Attie explained to Smythwick that Judie had to have her right leg "sawed off just below the knee" on December 31, 1937. That Judie survived the explosion and her surgery, "and has done as well as she has is the wonder of all her friends." Now that their niece Bertha was teaching high school, Attie noted that "most of the homework and nursing falls to me, and I am thankful for health and strength to do it." Along with caring for her sister, she also "had many invitations to talk on China," most of which she was able to accept.[9]

---

[6] Harriette King to Phil and Mattie Macon White, June 13, [1938], in the League, Attie T. Bostick folder, Foreign Mission Board Correspondence Collection (FMBCC), Box 33, Southern Baptist Historical Library and Archives (SBHLA), Nashville, TN.
[7] Ibid.
[8] Attie Bostick to Dear Friends, August 15, 1938.
[9] Attie Bostick to Gladys Smythwick, September 15, 1938.

The "burden" of Attie's "plea" during her church visits had "been for a good Christian Physician to" replace Mary King. Attie had heard that Smythwick had been considering a return to China, this time under appointment of the FMB. Because of Smythwick's mission experience and her knowledge of the Chinese language, Attie believed that the Pochow missionaries "would be very fortunate" to have her there: "I do not know how your health is, but we can ask and trust our kind Father to give you such health as you need for the work there. Do let us covenant together for this, claiming Jesus' promise 'where two agree on one thing' [Matt. 18:19]. . . . I shall send a copy of this [letter] to Dr. [Charles] Maddry, and I have a feeling I could get friends interested in paying your salary, if there is an agreement. Write me as to how you feel."[10] Attie's pleas for a missionary doctor apparently went unheeded, for the Southern Baptist *Annual* does not contain a reference to a missionary doctor being stationed at Pochow after 1936.

While Attie was attempting to secure a physician for Pochow, she was also trying to increase the number of missionaries at her station. Attie wrote Maddry, "begging" that he transfer Grace Stribbling, a missionary in Chengchow, to Pochow and reminding the corresponding secretary that Baptists were the only Protestants in Pochow. "I am hopeful of returning to China," she reported to Maddry, "but cannot make any plans yet, and I am trying daily to commit it all to Him who has promised to guide me 'with His eye upon me.'"[11] Eventually, Attie did return to Pochow, but Stribbling remained in Chengchow.

Attie's Preparation for Her Return to China

During 1939 the Japanese continued their occupation of three-fourths of the Southern Baptists' interior mission stations, with Chengchow being the only city under Chinese control. Florence Powell Harris, who was stationed in Kaifeng, provided the following information to the FMB in her report for the year:

> The middle class and poorer people have gradually drifted back to their homes in occupied areas, but on the whole, the student class, the intellectuals, and the wealthy ones who fled have not returned. Cities and hamlets in unoccupied areas continue to be bombed by invaders, thus causing much destruction to Baptist property. The lives of our missionaries have been miraculously spared during these perilous times. Traveling on railroads is made exceedingly dangerous by Chinese guerillas who also make raids on city suburbs and depots, causing anxiety and destruction. Bands of despera-

---

[10] Ibid. See also Attie Bostick to Charles Maddry, February 24, 1940.
[11] Attie Bostick to Charles Maddry, November 1, 1938. See Ps. 32:8, marg.

does, taking advantage of the present disturbed condition, swoop down on the poor farmer folk, taking their little. Thus the winter is faced with untold suffering among this people.[12]

In addition to these hardships, the missionaries at the Pochow station had no railroad service, which made transportation even more difficult. The Pochow missionaries also struggled in dealing with the effects of the famine. In August, Greene Strother led a famine relief effort for people living in the countryside. He found that the rains had brought flooding to many villages, with the wheat fields, millet fields, and truck gardens completely under water. The American Advisory Committee gave $85,000 and Southern Baptists gave $17,000 for famine relief. Despite the tremendous hardships the Chinese people were suffering, the Pochow missionaries' evangelistic efforts were rewarded: over 500 were baptized, a new building was purchased for a city church, a new church was organized, and the North River Church became self-supporting.[13]

By early 1939 Attie's sister Judie had completed a full year of recovering from her accident, but she still needed assistance with her personal care and was unable to cook or do housework. Bertha had been working as a music teacher to support herself and Judie, and Attie helped with the housework. In a February letter, Attie explained her situation to Jessie Ford, the woman who arranged transportation to China for Southern Baptist missionaries. Rather than sailing on the *Empress of Asia*, Attie asked if she could instead travel third class on the *Empress of Russia* and sail on September 16, her sixty-fourth birthday. "I have all the time wanted to return," she informed Ford,

> and my sister . . . wants me to return, but unless I can find someone to come into the home and do the work I am doing and about as well as I am doing it, I do not feel I can go and leave my sister and Brother G. P.'s second daughter [Bertha]. . . . It is not easy to find one who will undertake cooking, housekeeping and some nursing (my niece helps with this at night), for the amount we would be able to pay. I am paying into the running expenses $20.00 per month now and should feel I ought to continue that if I return, and the pay for the cook etc., would mostly need to come from me as my sister used up most of what she had in her four months in the Hospital and is paying Doctors. I hope you will not feel I am thrusting my home difficulties too much on you. I just wanted you to understand partly if later I must write and tell you to cancel my sailing.[14]

---

[12] *Annual*, SBC, 1940, 221.
[13] Ibid., 221-22.
[14] Attie Bostick to Jessie Ford, February 3, 1939.

Judie and Bertha Bostick, c.1939

Along with her letter, Attie sent Ford subscriptions she had procured for the FMB's magazine, *The Commission*. One man had amused Attie with his excuse for not subscribing: "'I cannot help you now, but hope later I can give you a donation,'" to which she responded: "'But I am not asking for a donation. I just want you to subscribe to our Foreign Mission magazine and inform yourself on our work.'"[15] Ford thanked Attie for the subscriptions and notified that her desire to travel third class on the *Empress of Russia* had been granted. Ford added, however, that she was "somewhat uneasy" about Attie's "comfort" in traveling third class.[16]

Apparently Attie found a good housekeeper for Judie, for she continued planning for her return to China. As the tension and conflict grew between Japan and Great Britain, she decided that it would be safer to sail to China on September 30 aboard the *Empress of Japan*, a Japanese ship.[17] Attie's travel plans changed, however, after Ford advised her that M. Theron Rankin, the FMB's secretary for the Orient, did not want her traveling third class. In a letter to Rankin, Attie explained that, being "a fair sailor," she considered traveling third class to "be the easiest way for me to help on the Debt this year. But since you and Miss Ford advise against this, I shall ask for second class" on a different ship.[18] Attie's plans changed again, but after securing her passport and making arrangements to have part of her salary sent to Judie and part sent to help reduce the FMB's debt, Attie boarded the *President Pierce* and sailed for China on October 2, 1939.[19]

---

[15] Ibid.
[16] Jessie Ford to Attie Bostick, February 17, 1939.
[17] For Attie's preparations for her return to China, see the following: Attie Bostick to Jessie Ford, August 8, 1939; Attie Bostick to Jessie Ford, August 22, 1939; and Attie Bostick to Jessie Ford, September 21, 1939.
[18] Attie Bostick to M. Theron Rankin, August 25, 1939.
[19] Attie Bostick to James Williams, October 3, 1939.

"Do you recognize all except the baby? Mai Ling is bright 'talkative' little thing—looks more western than Chinese. David has such a good ear for music. I hope he can have someone to help him. Jonathan is slow, more like his father. Hsi Hsin taught in the Kweiteh primary school last year while her husband studied in Kaifeng. The baby is a happy heart. She cares for it so well. Mrs. Meng was president of the W. M. S. in Kweiteh when I left."—Mattie M. White—"My cook, next his married daughter."— Attie Bostick, c. 1940

"The three Whites & I. I have on the colored voil, trimmed in ecru net & lace that Phil gave me, in all those." Attie Bostick, c. 1940

Attie's Return to Pochow, 1940

After arriving safely in China, Attie stayed with Mattie and Phillip White for several weeks in Kweiteh. Two Chinese delegations asked her to remain in Kweiteh, where she had served from January 1922 to September 1926 and then again from January 1931 to October 1932. She described for Jessie Ford how one person "suggested that my baggage should be held! I see the great need here and also know of the need at Pochow, but I told them I came out with the understanding I would go to Pochow, and though the suggestion was made, I am old enough and have been in the work long enough to decide this myself, and stay if I felt led to. I do not agree with this sugges-

"Ai Ts'um has an attractive personality. She was in Kaifeng last winter trying to get ready for regular Sr. High this fall. She seemed to be doing pretty well. Kweiteh is so weak on music. I wanted her to take as much piano as she could but the teacher had to leave during the first term. She wrote a happy letter about how she was blessed during the revival services this spring."--Mattie Macon White, c. 1940

"I think I sent one like this to Shelby so you may keep this, if you care to. It was taken in Martha's front yd. May 1940. Love, Attie."

tion unless it came from you friends in Richmond."[20] Being wanted in Kweiteh undoubtedly encouraged Attie, but she was soon off to the remote Pochow station and to the work and the people she loved.

Attie arrived in Pochow on February 13, 1940, to resume her work. Her Chinese friends welcomed her back and invited her to several feasts and celebrations, and she rejoiced that many people had become Christians while she was on furlough. Writing in coded language to Charles Maddry, Attie explained that a number of refugees had converted while they were in "the Two Camps": "A number joined our churches who received their impressions first in 'The Two Camps,' and are proving very helpful, proving over again Rom. 8:28."[21] This phrase refers to the North Yard and the South Yard, which were the two Baptist compounds that sheltered the Chinese refugees from the Japanese invaders during the fall of Pochow in May 1938. This ministry of providing a sanctuary, in addition to the famine relief that both the Baptists and the American Advisory Committee provided to the Chinese, helped to increase the number of converts. These ministries were for many Chinese the first contact they ever had with the missionaries.

---

[20] Attie Bostick to Jessie Ford, December 5, 1939.
[21] Attie Bostick to Charles Maddry, February 24, 1940. See also Attie Bostick to Mary King and Harriette King, March 2, 1940.

In a letter to Mary King and Harriette King, who were on furlough, Attie described some of the continuing ministries in Pochow, despite Japanese regulations:

> I am just back from seeing Mrs. Yang . . . and two young women who came with her from Ho Village, through the gates to enter Clifford's [Miss Barrett's] Class. This makes 73 I know who have come in for the Class and I imagine there are others I have not seen. The Japanese Guard at the gate actually smiled at me as I bowed in passing in! The people are groaning under the having to buy new passes, with their photos, taken by the one of their choice, costing at least .75 cts. One local young woman slipped in with us four and I felt rather to congratulate her than to object.[22]

The danger and stress of living in an occupied city did not consume Attie's attention. Although her letters during this time contain references to the occupation and its consequences, they are also filled with descriptions of normal, everyday affairs. For example, Attie thanked her sister-in-law Lena for money sent for the upkeep of the cemetery. G. P.'s headstone, "facing west as you may recall, is a part of the wall—no gate, but that gives the appearance of a gate, and we can see it from the house where you both lived, and where I am still staying with the Strothers." Attie then described the work being done on a house to which she would soon be moving. The price of wood had skyrocketed, forcing her to pay "the highest [price] any Bostick ever paid for wood I guess!"[23]

To her sister Judie, Attie expressed her thanks that all of Judie's letters had arrived safely:

"A Christian mother & her two sons. The Boy learning to walk."—Attie Bostick, c. 1940

---

[22] Attie Bostick to Mary King and Harriette King, March 2, 1940.
[23] Attie Bostick to Lena Bostick, March 8, 1940.

"I have indeed been fortunate in getting ALL your letters—twice each month." She also described for her sister some of the clothes she was wearing and how the remodeling of her home was progressing.[24]

In an April letter to Phil and Mattie White, Attie described some of the country work she had been doing:

> Your letters were taken out to the country by my rickshaw puller yesterday, and I read and enjoyed them as I rode in the dust and wind. Two women went out with me, and we were busy from early a.m. to a late bedtime. . . . This place, Chang Tientzi is only about nine miles out. Hue Ban used to go on his wheel on Sundays and hold meetings, and after he went to cook for you, my next cook did the same, and they spoke very appreciatively of the work both of them did. Tell your cook so. Years ago Wade had a small school of 21 pupils there, and now the one is the leader, and a consecrated man, Wang Sheo Teh is only the second of that number showing any interest in Christianity, but I told him I thought if he were the only one, the school had been very worthwhile. We had an early prayer meeting, went home and ate breakfast about eight. Then went back and studied, singing some for a rest and he taught the whole crowd a verse from a poster, and so we went till time to prepare and eat dinner. Again after dinner more study, till the ones from a distance had to leave. They eat supper out there, and we went back after supper, told our experiences, sang hymns we knew, since two lanterns did not light the little church enough to see to read much. Not many there can read, yet fifty or sixty were there studying most of the time. It made me feel we must cry to the Lord of the harvest for more laborers. I found these hungry faces—for learning coming up before me when I lay down on my comfortable bed for sleep last night![25]

Despite being able to continue her country work, getting to the outstations had become difficult for Attie. In a May letter she described for Judie the difficulty in traveling in rural China, noting that many of the roads had been dug out to prevent Japanese trucks from moving easily into the rural areas:

> Part of the country is still under Chinese rule, and to keep out trucks etc, the roads have been ditched right in the middle just like a very crooked worm had crawled through, as deep as a tall man. I was in a rickshaw, so the men could each carry the two conveyances across these places about a dozen times in making this not quite thirty miles. There are many small roads and they tried to go in these altogether, but there had to be some crossings, of these ditches, and there were some rivers to cross—bridges altogether demolished or so torn up that only a foot passenger could get across. I named my puller "Mr. Optimistic" for he was always hopeful of better roads ahead, or of a place to eat or drink tea! He was past fifty years of age, wearing an old straw hat and a patched pair of pants and a coat to match, all about the color of his old straw hat.[26]

---

[24] Ibid. See also Attie Bostick to Bertha Bostick, March 9, 1940.
[25] Attie Bostick to Phil and Mattie Macon White, April 21, 1940.
[26] Attie Bostick to Judie Bostick Eskridge, May 7, 1940.

On one trip Attie and two women spent eleven hours traveling in rickshaws some thirty miles to Ts'wei Low, a remote village. En route they were stopped three times by soldiers but were allowed to pass when the soldiers discovered that the women were missionaries. Along with the constant threat of being stopped by soldiers, the women had to endure hot, dusty traveling conditions. Eventually, Attie explained to Judie, "we finally let one of the men go to a village and offer to buy tea. It was hot and I much rather had cold water, but you know we feel it is not safe to drink the water from the wells here where there are so many graves and the wells uncovered most of the time, but I saw those two pullers go to the wells by the roadside time and again and drink water that had just been drawn. It was very hot and dusty and they could hardly have gone on pulling if they had not done that way."[27]

When the women arrived in Ts'wei Low, the villagers warmly welcomed them:

> The villagers brought out what tea they had ready and went and prepared more, and at the puller's request prepared six large bowls of "flour strings." The women and I did not eat any so they ate three each. I ate some boiled eggs and muffins I had carried along, and they some bread of that make. That wet tea did taste good, and the villages would not let us pay them for it. They said they formerly sold tea and eats by the roadside, but so few come and go, and buying and selling both restricted, they just shut up shop. I never saw so few people moving about in China on so long a trip before. We had four meetings a day, most of the time given to trying to teach them a small catechism that Mrs. [T. P.] Crawford got out years ago, 52 Bible verses that W.M.S. at Shanghai put out in a little booklet and we sell them for two cents. I took out forty and all were taken, and also other books. Some of the more advanced girls and women read Acts through at odd times while we were there. They certainly are keen on learning. I guess we had fifty and sixty most every day. Thursday it clouded up and we were so hopeful it would rain, but only a few drops fell.
>
> It was cooler the next day, and the clouds made it much easier for us. Poor old sisters!! I must have gone over The Six Salvation Tracts over one hundred times, and most of them still did not get them! There were two or three bright ones, a young girl or two and so they can go on and help them after I came away. They love Jesus and do "believe" as far as they know, but never having gone to school one day, and never having had anything but drudgery work around the home and farm, it was very hard for them to grasp and hold even the simplest truths. It seemed to me though when we came to a verse about Christ being nailed to a tree for our sins that they really got that so much quicker.

---

[27] Ibid.

Tell Mittie I think she will see some of the saved ones up in heaven, and that they will tell her how thankful they are that she is nursing you, and letting me work here.

They asked us to eat with them at noon each day. The first day a church member had a guest she wanted us to meet. The next day the Church members went in together and some forty ate together. They caught and killed a fish they had been feeding in a nearby pond that weighed 11 catties—a little over fourteen lbs.! They said the water had dried up once and they thought the fish was finished, but later when there was water, it came back! Sounds "fishy," doesn't it?[28]

The Japanese occupation had caused inflation and left many people homeless. Nevertheless, as Attie described for Jessie Ford, the missionary work continued:

We are trying to dispense the help that has come out for the needy, and as we approach wheat harvest (in about half a month) times get more tense. Grain is not permitted to be brought in this J.[Japanese]-owned, no-ruled territory, so it is $3.00 per bushel, the highest it has ever been known to be, and stalks to cook their food with are exorbitant in price. Yet the country I passed through last week had an abundance of fuel stored on their threshing floors. They always pick up hope though just before wheat harvest, and many who had left homes because of floods, etc, are now trying to get back to their own places to help gather wheat. I saw whole families on the road, the small ones and their few things on a barrow, and the older ones trudging along in the heat. We have a few schools for the ones who want to study the Gospel, and feed the one hundred who have been carefully selected. One of our old members came before I was downstairs this a.m., to ask if my cook (a trusty church member, who had a while studying in Mr. Gillespie's Bible School) might go and help with this work for the next twelve days. After consultation with Mrs. Strother, I was glad to let him go, and plan to have my noon meals with the Strothers. My gardener and I can easily manage breakfast and supper, since I eat very simply at both these. My cook had two months with the preaching band this spring, and has just been home a week, but I found him and the gardener busy canning cherries when I got in Saturday. The eleven quarts and one pint will be nice to have next winter.[29]

In a letter to Attie, Ford had assured her that the FMB staff constantly prayed for her and her co-workers. To a fervent woman of prayer such as Attie, Ford's words were comforting: "Today is our Women's Prayer Meeting, at eleven o'clock, and I plan to go so must sign off. You cannot know how much it means to us that you think of and pray for us. We try to do the same for you."[30]

---
[28] Ibid.
[29] Attie Bostick to Jessie Ford, May 8, 1940
[30] Ibid.

Increased Fighting

In July 1940 the fighting between the Chinese and the Japanese intensified in Pochow because the Chinese were trying to retake the city. "We seem always to have war with us here," Attie lamented in a letter to Charles Maddry. "'The visiting team' [Japanese soldiers] are shut up in our City the past four days and nights, and each night we have heard guns and machine guns. The bridge a little southeast of us, crossing Wade's 'Million Dollar View,' was set on fire night before last but burned only a short while as it has just been recently completed with unseasoned timbers that do not bother to burn fast. The original one, fine Oregon pine completed just a little more than three years ago was destroyed in the first invasion."[31]

The sound of gunfire and the humid temperatures made sleeping difficult for Attie, but the Japanese were also experiencing problems. Chinese guerrillas were attempting to retake occupied territory, "covering eight nearby counties, and so outside help has not reached 'them' [the Japanese] so readily as in former days. A number of Chinese soldiers, trained for months by 'them,' turned to their own when they got this opportunity." The Chinese Christians anticipated demonstrations and looting the evening of July 4 and asked to take refuge in Attie's cellar, which she assured them that they could. Attie told her friends:

> I was not hiding things, but would not object to their things being out here but could not insure them. I had provided some of 'their' money with the thought of going to Korea with Mrs. Strother, but after we decided Mr. Strother should go instead, I spent it along when needed. It had been at a premium, but now no one wants it. We have been permitted to use both kinds here all along, but at Kweiteh 'they' guarded carefully that former currency should not be used in business, even searching the stores and persons for it. I shall not regret burning the $60.00 I have still on hand, if 'they' get out![32]

In the midst of fighting, Attie maintained her faith by relying on two of her favorite passages, Romans 8:28 and Isaiah 26:3:

> We . . . have Rom. 8:28 to fall back on, and I know we love the Lord, and so with many other unexplainable mysteries during my past life, I am thankful to leave it with Him.
>
> As we stood around my sister's bedside last Sept. 27th, and each of us quoted a verse of Scripture, Estelle [Wade's wife], quoted Isa. 26:3—"Thou wilt keep him in perfect peace whose mind is stayed on Thee; because he

---

[31] Attie Bostick to Charles Maddry, July 4, 1940.
[32] Ibid.

trusteth in Thee." It has always been a favorite of mine, but very specially since I arrived in China this time, and as bullets whistle by (mostly toward the City and NOT toward this suburb) that verse has time and again come to my mind.

Despite the whistling bullets, Attie assured Maddry that God's word continued to be spread: "I had three trips into the country in the spring and greatly enjoyed them. People are so keen to learn more of God's word, and a great interest is manifested everywhere, 'and there are many adversaries.'"[33]

Maddry later wrote to Attie, empathizing with her and the Chinese people, but also encouraging her:

> First of all let, me express my sincere sympathy with you and the other dear missionaries in the light of all the severe trials through which you are passing in China at this time. I shall always remember with a great deal of delight the quiet and the charm of the home visit I had with you and Wade at Pochow when I was in China. It is hard to realize that now for these many months China has been so rent asunder by this terrible war. Chinese people have suffered untold misery and agony and the strain on our missionaries, I am sure, has been severe beyond words to express. . . .
>
> I still have faith, however, to believe that China will win this struggle eventually and that gracious and blessed peace will come to the Orient. I am praying earnestly for that time to come. In the meantime we are going to do our best to send recruits to both Japan and China and get ready for the glorious new day for the Gospel that will surely come in both of these stricken lands in God's own good time.[34]

In 1940 the conflict between the Chinese and the Japanese military increased, prompting the United States State Department to issue an urgent warning for all Americans, including missionaries, to evacuate the country immediately. Many missionaries left China in November 1940. Greene and Martha Strother evacuated Pochow because they were scheduled for a furlough in the spring of 1941. Mattie White, her two children, and Olive Riddell left Kweiteh, leaving Phil White and Grace Stribling to continue the work there. Attie and Miss Clifford Barratt stayed on as the only Southern Baptist missionaries in Pochow. In October the Southern Baptist Convention Board of Directors had voted unanimously to allow Attie to continue her work in China; however, word of the vote did not reach her until four months later, after she had already decided to stay. Lois Prossor, an associate missionary not appointed by the FMB, also remained in Pochow.

---

[33] Ibid.
[34] Charles Maddry to Attie Bostick, September 6, 1940.

In November 1940 Barratt contracted yellow jaundice, and after seeking treatment in Pochow and Kweiteh, she went to Peking, where she began to improve. Thus, Attie was the only Baptist missionary in Pochow from December 26, 1940, until March 12, 1941.[35]

Despite the war the Pochow station experienced numerous successes in 1940, with 596 people being baptized, and 610 pledging to tithe. Moreover, at the annual November association meeting, the country churches called their own evangelists and pledged to support them with funds or produce.[36]

As the conflict between Japan and China continued to intensify, missionaries from the northern parts of China traveled south toward "Free China." En route, some stopped at Pochow to stay with Attie until they could assemble their baggage and additional transportation for the trip south. She hosted twenty-five people, including three children. Because Kweiteh was more accessible by train, many more stayed with Phil White, who provided refuge to over 100 missionaries until the Japanese stopped their movement in early 1941.

During these months conditions in China grew worse, as floods damaged crops and the Japanese military destroyed food supplies.[37] In her April 1941 letter to L. C. Hylbert, treasurer of the American Advisory Committee in Shanghai, Attie described the difficulties in China that had been caused by the flooding of the Yellow River on August 15, 1940. The river had recently overflowed again, which again ruined the wheat crop. These problems were partly caused by the poor maintenance of the dykes under Japanese control.[38]

Attie also described for Hylbert an incident in which Japanese soldiers detained Lois Prossor, Pastor Chao, and others, who had left Pochow on bikes and had $10,000 in relief funds:

> About 300 soldiers met them with guns, had them hold up their hands and move some feet away from their wheels, asked what they had, but were told the truth, and were permitted to go on and see the magistrate. Some of the soldiers were not happy to lose such an opportunity of obtaining so nice a sum, and remarked in the hearing of some of our other folk: "Why did we let them go? We could have shot them all, taken the money, and no one would have been left to tell the tale." An official replied, "Take money belonging to the Christians—no we cannot do that." I feel sure our Master kept them in this exposure.[39]

---

[35] Attie Bostick to Miss Newton, March 25, 1941.
[36] *Annual,* SBC, 1941, 247.
[37] Attie Bostick to Miss Newton, March 25, 1941.
[38] Attie Bostick to L. C. Hylbert, April 24, 1941.
[39] Ibid.

That evening, robbers entered the home where Prossor was staying and shined a light in her face, asked who she was, and then left with $300 worth of cloth. Of course, the Japanese official could have ordered the murder of the Christians and taken their money, and the robbers could have done much more to the vulnerable Miss Prosser than just ask who she was. But they did not, and Attie was convinced that the Lord had protected them all, for she proclaimed to Hylbert: "Our God IS ABLE."[40]

In her letter of May 5, 1941, Attie described for Judie how the Japanese military was trying to prevent people from fleeing to "Free China":

> You see "The outside team" [Japanese military] does all they can to keep people and THINGS out of "Free China." A party of 20, from Shantung came in last week—going west to preach and work. Pastor Feng, a Chinese Baptist, . . . preached for us yesterday, and mentioned that so many different units had come into their Community he decided he wanted to go west where the need is greater. He must be past fifty, children and grandchildren in this party of 20, and so as in the early church, persecution is spreading the Gospel. It was fine for Grace [Stribling] to have their company, and for them to have hers. My Gardener went with them till they were in "free" country, and said they got along o.k. He has been several times, and the guards know him. They were halted and told they could not proceed (and that is really the "orders"), but when they saw him, they were told to go forward. There were 12 carts, pulled by men. Grace had another beside the one she was on—both well-loaded.[41]

Attie also recounted for Judie a tense situation with a Japanese soldier who had searched her home in the fall of 1940. He returned in the spring of 1941, but this time he was drunk. Two of Attie's fellow missionaries, Clifford Barratt and Grace Stribling, along with three Chinese teachers and a child, were in Attie's sitting room when the soldier arrived. Sensing the potential danger of the situation, two male Chinese Christians, Mr. Pien and David Yang, entered the room and stayed with Attie and her friends until the soldier left, taking with him some gospel tracts Attie had given to him.[42]

The Deaths of Mrs. Su and Philip White

On July 3, 1941, Mrs. Su, a faithful Bible woman, died of cancer, only two weeks after the death of her husband. She had worked for the Baptist missionaries since January 1929 and had proclaimed the gospel to many of her

---

[40] Ibid.
[41] Ibid.
[42] Ibid.

countrymen and women. Mrs. Su was the mother of David Yang, the principal of the Baptist School in Pochow. Her death was a loss for Attie and the other Christians in Pochow. Yang recently had felt the call to preach and was accepted at the University in Shanghai, which he planned to attend in the fall. After Attie heard him preach one Sunday in 1937, she "prayed most earnestly that God would call him into His special service. . . . I was dead earnest, too. Yet," as she confessed to Charles Maddry, "when he told me of his call this spring my first question was 'How will our school get along without you?' Such is our weak human nature!!"[43]

Attie suffered another personal loss on September 11, 1941, when Phil White died after an appendix operation.[44] She alluded to White's death in her letter of November 4, 1941, to Maddry, stating that "Phil went Home." Attie praised White, describing him as "a good leader, full of faith and love."[45]

After White's death, Attie decided to move to Kweiteh in order to assist Christians at that mission station. As she explained to Maddry, traveling to the Kweiteh outstations was uncomfortable, but the reception she was receiving and the progress of the gospel made the trips worthwhile:

> Riding on the open truck, in an open dust storm, the dust a foot deep in many places, is not enough fun to go every day, but each time I go the first question that greets me is, "Have you come to stay?" I was at the Teacher's prayer meeting, in my own home both nights I went down, and was helped by the contacts. They are fine teachers and I love them all. Pastor Chao came in style—the two hundred yards to my home, on a wheelbarrow. He has been suffering some weeks from an in-growing nail, and young Sun Pao Ching is treating it, but one who has had such knows it is very painful. The next day, Saturday was "Young Peoples Day" in our church, and I attended the first part, in our First Baptist Church, which has been enlarged, but the first floor was full. The City Church and also the North River, no the North Suburb joined in the meeting. They elected new officers for the coming year, and I wish you might have seen the enthusiasm for which they voted for Mr. Yang, only nineteen [years old] who came this fall from Kaifeng to help teach. He had really come from Pingtu, to attend our High School in Kaifeng, but was willing to help us out when the appeal went up there. Our students looked upon him questioningly when he arrived—so young, but the way three hundred hands shot up, voting him as their leader, we could see he had won their confidence and love. One of our own boys who graduated last June from old Brother Ke's church, and is now principal of the city school, received the next highest vote. Their singing was good, and I am thankful this young Dr. Sun is taking up the place of organist, and

---

[43] Attie Bostick to Charles Maddry, July 5, 1941.
[44] Handwritten note concerning Philip E. White, in the White, Philip E. folder, FMBCC, Box 63, SBHLA.
[45] Attie Bostick to Charles Maddry, November 4, 1941.

is helping train the singers. The enthusiastic spirit is "catching," and does one good.[46]

Attie's November letter to Maddry was the last she wrote before the Japanese attacked Pearl Harbor, Hawaii, on December 7, 1941. The consequences of that attack would directly affect Attie and her fellow missionaries.

---

[46] Ibid.

Chapter Seven

ATTIE'S YEARS OF INTERNMENT
1941-1943

*Being confident of this very thing, that he which hath begun
a good work in you will perform it until the day of Jesus Christ. (Phil. 1:6)*

Attie's Internment in the Kweiteh Lutheran Compound

In her letter of January 21, 1936, to Charles Maddry and his wife, Attie described some of her future plans. She had purchased "a cottage on the mountain . . . to go to in the summer, with a thought I may 'retire' there later" in "this land of my adoption."[1] Five years later, however, events half way around the world would alter Attie's dreams.

In the early morning hours of December 7, 1941, Japan attacked the United States' Pacific fleet at Pearl Harbor, Hawaii. This surprise attack damaged all eight U. S. Battleships, sunk five of them, and killed over 2,400 people.[2] The attack signaled not only a new phase in the war raging around the globe; it also signaled Japan's new policy toward missionaries serving in China, which had been occupied by the Japanese army since 1937.

The Japanese executed a highly coordinated, well-planned attack, in which they bombed Pearl Harbor and simultaneously captured American missionaries and business people who were living in territory occupied by Japan. Attie was living in occupied China and was taken into custody by the Japanese military on December 8, 1941.[3] She was one of the Southern Baptist missionaries arrested by the Japanese authorities, who interned her and several others in the Lutheran compound in Kweiteh. Those interned with Attie were her cook; Nurse Kelsey; two Catholic sisters; Mr. and Mrs. Ditminson and their fifteen-year-old son; Miss Regiew; Miss Schmidt; Miss Quiring; Degarmo; and the "Mingling party," which included the Mennonite missionary Loyal Bartel, his aunt, and her coworker, Miss Reglar. The "Mingling party" had been in Ming Ling for the Sunday church service on December 7 and were arrested the following day.[4]

---

[1] Attie Bostick to Charles and Mrs. Maddry, January 21, 1936.
[2] Edward Davidson and Dale Manning, *Chronology of World War Two* (New York: Sterling Publishing Co., 2000), 91.
[3] Because China is on the opposite side of the International Dateline, the attack on Pearl Harbor occurred on the morning of December 8 in China.
[4] Attie Bostick, "Diary of the Concentration Camp, 1941-1942, Lutheran Compound, Kweiteh, Honan," in the League, Attie T. Bostick folder, Foreign Mission Board Correspondence Collection (FMBCC), Box 33, Southern Baptist Historical Library and Archives (SBHLA), Nashville, TN.

Two Baptist missionaries, Hannah Sallee and Josephine Ward, both of Kaifeng, were placed under guard in house arrest in the Drum Tower Church compound in the home formerly occupied by the Harris family. Three other women missionaries remained in their respective cities: Katie Murray and Grace Stribling in Chengchow, and Addie Cox in Wei Shih.[5]

At the Lutheran compound in Kweiteh, Attie and Nurse Kelsey were assigned to one bedroom, while the Ditminsons stayed in the room next to them. The following day, December 9, Lois Prossor and Clifford Irene Barratt were brought from Pochow to the compound, and the Catholic sisters were allowed to return to their convent. Later that day the Thiessens were also brought to the compound. By December 9, 1941, at least fifteen people resided in the Lutheran compound.

Attie's Internment Diary

While interned, Attie kept a diary with brief entries, listing some of her daily activities. Following are some of her diary entries:

- Dec. 10-Settling down.

- Dec. 11-The military called. They took down several abilities.

- Dec. 12-Rather cold. We started playing games in the evening.

- Dec. 13-Saturday. We cleaned up, beating the rugs. Breakfast 8:30. Devotions, men cut wood, exercise, study, 1:00 o'clock soup, reading and games. Supper, singing and devotions, games.

- Dec. 14-Sunday, first service, Bro. Ditminson preached on "Do not worry for the morrow."

- Dec. 15-Monday, wash day. They came after Bro. Ditminson's radio.

- Dec. 16-They took two tins of oil and thanked Bro. Ditminson for it.

- Dec. 17-Beautiful day. Hair washing. Bro. Bartel gave first testimony. Following this, one testimony was given each evening.

- Dec. 18-Mr. Bartel received word from Ts'so Msien.

---

[5] *Annual*, Southern Baptist Convention (SBC), 1942, 227-30.

- Dec. 19-Miss Barratt gave her testimony.

- Dec. 20-Lovely day. We shelled peanuts and made candy.

- Dec. 21-Sunday. Mr. Bartel preached on Ps. 46. "The God of Jacob." John Wieneke came.

- Dec. 22-Monday. Wash day. Preparations were made for Christmas.

- Dec. 23-Monday. Guards were changed. [The Guards] got drunk and went upstairs in the night.

- Dec. 24-Mr. Bartel had news from Ts'ao Hsien about the family being moved into the city. The police dog came.

- Dec. 25-Christmas morning. Oranges for breakfast, and a present at everybody's plate. Decorations of red paper and sweets given to guards. Bro. Thiessen gave Christmas message. Had a big chicken dinner, with fruit cake, apples, oranges and candy. Hymn singing-carols.

- Dec. 26-North wind snow and cold—put up the little stove in the dining room. Reading and games.

- Dec. 27-Thiessens got their money from the military. News that Hsien Hin Ruel have taken over the churches and a Japanese doctor coming to the hospital. Prayer meeting.

- Dec. 28-Sunday. Mr. Ditminson led the service. More exciting news about churches.

- Dec. 29-Monday. Another beautiful day. . . .

- Dec. 30-Studied. Guard changed. More old groups returned. Had scripture on Holy Spirit. New Testament.

- Dec. 31-Was a beautiful day. . . . Chinese dinner. Heard about Miss [?] plans to go to free China.

- Jan. 1, 1942-Still in camp. Had late breakfast and then prayer. Dinner at 3 p.m. My verse for the year Phil. 1:6.

- Jan. 2-Studied. Had prayer meeting. Took bath in the evening.

- Jan. 3-Cleaned a little. Was "second boy." Ira helped. Had prayer meeting.

- Jan. 4-Sunday. Bro. Bartel preached on Elijah. Heard news from kitchen people that report is out that we have our ears cut off and the men's heads are cut off!

- Jan. 5-Washed. Had prayer meeting. Finished our study of the Holy Spirit. Guard changed. Had picture taken of our group at camp.

- Jan. 6-Studied. Started study of Psalms, reading them in Chinese and English. Officers came. We requested for cheque books. They said soon we would be released.

- Jan. 7-Studied. Had last day of prayer meeting. Had butter from Olsons. Received shoes from Evangelist Yang of Liu Ho. Bro. Bartel received some clothes and a verse from "Susan," his wife. Officers brought news, saying they would soon have the White House [in Washington, DC]!

- Jan. 8-Wrote letter. Bro. Thiessen had a tumble outside. Was rather windy. Started reading Dan Matthews, by H.B. Wright, aloud.

- Jan. 9-Chinese had meeting outside with authorities. Studying of language and also Psalms.

- Jan. 10-Studied. Cleaned some. Study of Psalms. Rather cold all day.

- Jan. 11-Sunday. Bro. Thiessen preached on the Star of Bethlehem. Read and sang in the evening.

- Jan. 12-Guards changed. Washed. Studied. Beautiful day. Psalms studied.

- Jan. 13-Studied. Psalms studied. Daily walk and ball playing. Guard came up and took some guards off.

- Jan. 14-Studied. Psalms studied. Prayer meeting. Miss Kelsey washed her hair.

- Jan. 16-Washed hair and took bath. Officials came early. Dr. Hsu came in. . . . W. to see Miss Prossor. Officials came also. A beautiful sunshiny day. Received butter and regards from Olsons.

- Jan. 17-Cleaned. Miss Bostick washed her hair. Study of Psalms. And another beautiful day. Bro. Bartel had visitor, was student.

- Jan. 18-Sunday. Bro. Ditminson preached. Hot tea in A.M. & in evening one of the guards got excited because of the lights we were burning.

- Jan. 19-Monday. Guards did not change. Received our check books and things, but not Miss DeGarmo's drafts. Dr. Hsu sent a nice big fish for dinner. In P.M. four officials came, but did not say much. Wall behind the house built up.

- Jan. 20-Guards changed. Prayer meeting. Studied some. The men got a month-old paper. Quite a joke. Had some stomach pains and Miss Schmidt was sick in the night. Studied. Two officials came and gave report of two American boats sunk, etc.

- Jan. 22-Hsu Pa Sao stayed in bed this morning. Iris dreamt of bottles falling out of bed. We decided to make a . . . cartoon of marching with our water bottles.

- Jan. 23-Studied some. Bath. Was nice and warm.

- Jan. 24-Studied. Played ball with Ira. . . Had Psalm study on porch upstairs. Took long walk with Miss Kelsey in the yard. . . .[6]

Attie's Internment at Phil White's Home in Kweiteh

On January 31, 1942, after spending fifty-five days in the Lutheran compound, the Japanese permitted many of the internees to return to their previous homes to await further instructions. Attie and her cook returned to Phil White's house, the place in which she had been residing in Kweiteh following White's death in September 1941. During their time in the compound, most captives did not write letters nor did they receive correspondence. Shortly after returning to White's residence, Attie wrote

---

[6] Bostick, "Diary of the Concentration Camp, 1941-1942." Note: the entries for the last days are missing.

her first letter home. On February 5, 1942, she described for her "precious Sister, Judie," her time in the compound. Attie explained that on December 8, 1941, she received several letters from home that were filled with newspaper clippings. Because mail delivery had been irregular since the Japanese invasion in 1937, she was eager to catch up on the news from home. After she had finished reading a letter from Judie and had begun reading the newspaper clippings, she was called to eat the noon meal. Attie described for Judie what happened after the meal: "Just as I was finishing my noon meal, some callers came and I got ready to move into Mr. Ditminson's 'more easily protected' in the City."[7] The "callers" were Japanese soldiers, whom Attie cryptically referred to as "They": "'They' asked me if I wanted my cook to go [to the Lutheran compound]. 'I should very much like him to go if he is willing. I do not want to compel him to go.' Then he was asked if he cared to go. 'She is my mistress and if she wants me to go, then I shall go.' So he cooked for the 13 of us and I looked after the household some, the women took turns setting the table and receiving the food from the kitchen through the little window that opened into the kitchen, also cleaned house."[8]

Attie and her fellow internees lived with constant uncertainty. The Japanese soldiers controlled the missionaries' lives and their movements. They could make no plans for their future and were not allowed to write letters or communicate with anyone outside their compound. Despite being interned, Attie and her fellow missionaries refused to give into despair. "It was like a religious conference with us," she explained to Judie. "We sang many good old hymns after each meal. Prayer after breakfasts, and after supper scripture reading and study. We observed the week of Prayer in January. Each Sunday we met in the dining room and one of the three men led services for us."[9]

Perhaps the hardest day for everyone at the compound was Christmas. Attie described the special treat of oranges for breakfast and a present at everyone's plate on Christmas day. She admitted that she had given up hope of ever being able to return to White's home and felt that her return was a gift from God:

> It was good to see "home" again, for I think I had given it up during these [55] days, so it was like getting it again from my kind Father. Not a flower had died, but there were a few dead leaves. "They" had opened up the house only once for the gardener to water them. They [Chinese Christians] seem more like friends now than ever and I am thankful for them. I sent one

---

[7] Attie Bostick to Judie Bostick Eskridge, February 5, 1942. This letter has inserts by Estelle Bostick, Attie's sister-in-law. Estelle added, "The callers were evidently the Japanese taking her to the Lutheran Compound."
[8] Ibid. See also Attie Bostick to Loved Ones, April 2, 1942.
[9] Attie Bostick to Judie Bostick Eskridge, February 5, 1942.

pot in to the Interpreter who came several times here and to our "Conference,"[10] on business matters. We received no letters or papers, and I wrote none. Miss Barratt did write Dr. Williams and word has come he received it. But we felt there was very little hope of getting any letters to you, but praise the Lord, the way to His Throne was and is open and we prayed often for you.[11]

Despite the military domination by the Japanese, the internment of missionaries, and the sealing of the churches, the Chinese Christians had continued to meet in their homes. These Christians, Attie informed Judie, had taken "over the support of the work, which we have been trying to encourage for years. Rom. 8:28 has been a constant comfort and we feel this is indeed 'working together for our good.'" The Chinese Christians also had collected money and food to help the internees. Attie described their kindness, which affected her deeply: "last Saturday . . . Pien Hsiang Hsin, Hsu, and David Yang came from Pochow to Kweiteh to see me and brought me fifty dollars to help out at this time. My eyes filled with tears." Pastor Chung had also sent apples, and every day Attie's gardener had brought milk to the internees.[12]

After being released from the Lutheran compound, Attie also wrote to Mr. Ditminson, a fellow internee, describing her return to Phil White's house. Japanese soldiers had visited the home and asked her if anything was missing: "I did and mentioned the cook's watch, but he was generous to say it was not a very good one and so they need not to bother. After closer looking, I miss[ed] Phil's camera and his warm winter gloves, a few other things including my finger nail scissors, [and] Phil's desk scissors."[13]

Attie then wrote to her fellow missionaries in Pochow, Clifford Barrett and Lois Prossor, asking them to check on her home in Pochow to see if anything had been stolen, and if so, she hoped that the Japanese might return the items. She also expressed her thanks that the two women were safe together, and described her trip to the hospital for some tests: "Yesterday I asked for permission to go to Hospital for an X Ray, and to my delight and surprise, obtained it. . . . I went at 3 p.m. yesterday, returned at ten this a.m. The police here seem quite nice—one rode in a rickshaw behind me to Hospital and one from over there came home with me today. Of course I paid the fare. Nothing very radically wrong as seen by the X-Ray, but Drs. suggested certain cathartics for my bowels."[14]

---

[10] The "conference" was the internment in the Lutheran compound. See the note inserted in Attie Bostick to Mr. Tewinkle, February 11, 1942.
[11] Attie Bostick to Judie Bostick Eskridge, February 5, 1942.
[12] Ibid. See also Attie Bostick to L. C. Hylbert, March 26, 1942.
[13] Attie Bostick to Brother Ditminson, n.d.
[14] Attie Bostick to Clifford Barratt and Lois Prossor, n.d.

In her letter to L. C. Hylbert, treasurer of the American Advisory Committee in Shanghai, Attie reported on how she had spent funds for the Kweiteh mission. More importantly, however, she described the kindness with which several Chinese Christians had shown her: "Last week an evangelist WALKED in twenty miles and brought me sixty eggs. His congregation had given money to buy them and send them to me. Yesterday a young man, also twenty miles out, started in with thirty-one, but broke eleven as he brought them, carefully wrapped in paper, on his bike. The roads are rough! Pastor Tung's mother brought me forty eggs and such a nice pomegranate when she came back from her new year's visit to her daughter, living out in the country. She is past eighty and came by wheelbarrow."[15]

As Attie, her cook, and his wife continued to live in Phil White's former home, they did what they could to assist each other and the other missionaries. The gardener at White's home took a quart of milk each day to Mr. Ditminson, who was still confined in the Lutheran compound, and he in turn provided news to Attie and her household.

Attie was quite proud of her cook, who had faithfully served everyone in the Lutheran compound and had proven to be a strong Christian. She praised him in a letter to "Loved Ones" back home in Shelby, North Carolina:

> All were pleased with his work and faithfulness, and I think he has grown spiritually because of this experience. He has been Pastor Chung's right hand man since we came back—leading a service nearly every Sunday as the congregation part met in a home in this suburb, and part in the City in homes. But praise the Lord, the church was opened March 31, [1942], and the folk can meet there. There were 46 sisters at p.m. yesterday, my cook's wife reported, and in the p.m. they met men and all, and elected officers for the coming year, especially for the Sunday School. We are so thankful the literature has come for this and the Woman's Missionary Union.[16]

Attie, who remained under house arrest by the Japanese in White's home, was not allowed to attend church services. So, for Easter, she sent some geraniums to attend "in my place."

Attie comforted her loved ones by assuring them that she was fine. "I feel you have not worried over me, and am so thankful," she reassured them. "My every need has been supplied. 'His eye is on the sparrow' and I know He cares for me."[17]

---

[15] Attie Bostick to L. C. Hylbert, March 26, 1942.
[16] Attie Bostick to Loved Ones, April 2, 1942.
[17] Ibid.

Attie's Move to the Hospital Compound in Kweiteh

The spring of 1942 brought hopes of repatriation for three of the remaining missionaries—Attie, Miss Kelsey, and one other. Attie was preparing mentally to sail for the United States, but on June 7, she learned that there was no room on the boat. Instead of leaving for home, she would be moved instead to the Canadian Episcopal Hospital Compound in Kweiteh. In a letter written on June 13, 1942, to Bishop Ochoe, she described waiting for Japanese soldiers to come to White's home, and make a record of the household goods before they took her to the hospital compound. She offered the Bishop the opportunity to come and select any furniture he wanted before the soldiers arrived.[18]

Attie arrived at the hospital on June 20, 1942. During her internment there, she had relatively more freedom than she previously had at the Lutheran compound, where she had been under surveillance, and denied any visitors, including the Chinese Christians who had tried to contact her. Attie walked around the compound without an escort, and she even returned twice to White's house, alone. A policeman guarded the hospital's entrance, but he paid little attention to the internees.[19]

Attie considered her move to the hospital to be a two-fold blessing: she enjoyed the "constant fellowship" of Nurse Kelsey, with whom she roomed, and "of course [it] is cheaper."[20] While living in the hospital, Attie naturally turned her thoughts to the spiritual work that needed to be done in China. One of her main concerns centered on the continuation of the work she and other Baptists had begun in Pochow and in Kweiteh. In a letter to Mary Alexander, a fellow missionary in Shanghai, Attie wrote: "I have not been in our church [in Kweiteh] since last December 7. Pastor Chung has been a great strength and help during these months, and I am so thankful Phil [White] got him ordained before he passed away. They say all the churches are unsealed now, for which I am most thankful. I mean here, and in the country around, but the last I heard from Kaifeng two of ours were still sealed. The Episcopal Bishop Cheng has been a great help in all these churches, and said he was still working to try and get the two of ours in K[aifeng] opened. The church members are doing remarkably well in supporting their leaders."[21] Although she did not know when she would return to the United States, Attie maintained her faith by trusting her future "to Him who cares for the sparrows."[22]

---

[18] Attie Bostick to Bishop Ochoe, June 13, 1942.
[19] Attie Bostick to Grace Stribling, June 25, 1942.
[20] Attie Bostick to Mary Alexander, July 6, [1942].
[21] Ibid.
[22] Ibid., [P.S]. See also Attie Bostick to Miss Wang, a Chinese Bible Woman, July 15, 1942.

Because the Japanese censored many letters, missionaries circulated their correspondence in a round-robin fashion to those who were able to get letters out of occupied China. This process enabled Attie to send information to her family in North Carolina.[23] Receiving information from home, however, proved to be difficult. During the first two months of her internment in the Canadian Episcopal Hospital in Kweiteh, Attie received no letters from home. Finally, in early August 1942, she received a letter addressed in Chinese that contained a letter written by Judie on February 2, 1942. The next day Attie received two letters from her brother Wade and his wife, Estelle. In a letter to "Loved Ones," Attie expressed her delight at receiving much cherished news from home. She was so excited that she had literally jumped for joy:

> Solomon says, "As cold waters to a thirsty soul, so is good news from a far country" [Prov. 25:25], and I heartily agree with him. I was so delighted to open a letter, addressed in Chinese and find Judie's of February 2 enclosed that I think I really did some jumping up and down! Then yesterday came the one of March 3, with Wade's and 'Stelle's, and today still another of Wade's and his wife's. Thank you all SO MUCH! Judie's of February 16 mentions she did not get it finished the day before, but that sheet is all that came. Maybe the other was in another letter.[24]

Attie informed her family that she had not been among those who had left China on previous ships. She also told her family that she, Mr. Ditminson, and Nurse Kelsey had been notified that they would leave in two months or perhaps even earlier. Such news, however, thrilled neither Attie nor Kelsey, for they asked "to remain, but we had asked that before and were refused, so we will likely be required to go, if the Steam Ship takes others." After providing news about Ditminson and Clifford Barratt, Attie described for her family the weather, the crops, and her daily walks with Kelsey. Attie's appetite was good, and she notified her family that, by not having to pay any servants, she was saving money.[25]

Part of the last paragraph of Attie's letter to her family contained these words: "We asked Mr. Ditminson for supper Saturday Night to celebrate Judie's 81st birthday [August 1], and had special prayer for her. Maybe I'll get there before she does! It is all in our Father's loving care, and Rom. 8:28 is my constant comfort. Dearest love to you and all, especially those who pray for me."[26]

---

[23] See Mary Alexander to Attie Bostick, Grace Stribling, Kattie Murray, and Addie Cox, July 28, 1942.
[24] Attie Bostick to Loved Ones in Shelby, NC, August 3, 1942. This letter was sent first to Grace Stribling, who then sent it to Shelby.
[25] Ibid.
[26] Ibid.

The Death of Attie's Beloved Sister Judie

On August 18, 1942, Attie's beloved sister Judie died. She had supported Attie's dream of becoming a missionary when Attie first received her call to missions, and she had faithfully written Attie twice a month while her sister lived in China. Just a month before Judie's death, Attie expressed her astonishment at her sister's devotion in a letter written on July 15, 1942, to Grace Stribling: "Judie IS remarkable in her letter writing especially when you consider she never attended school but three months in her life."[27] Judie had also supported Attie financially until her nearly fatal water heater accident in December 1937. Such devotion caused Attie, in an interview several years after she returned to the United States, to declare: "Three of us Bosticks went to China as missionaries, but my sister Judie was the finest missionary of us all, and she never left the homeland or knew a well day."[28] Despite the great distance that separated them, Attie always remained close to Judie.

Attie's niece Bertha Bostick, who lived with and cared for Judie, wrote a letter on August 27, 1942, in which she described Judie's final days. As her health began to deteriorate, Judie suffered severe pain and could hardly stand to be touched. According to Bertha, "On Saturday, two weeks after her birthday, she went into a complete coma; and all the lines of pain and suffering left her face, and she just lay for those four days, peacefully breathing her life away, breathing and pulse growing weaker until the last breath at one-twenty Wednesday morning, August 19."[29] Bertha's letter was sent to a number of friends and relatives in the States. It was then sent overseas to Katie Murray, who forwarded it to Grace Stribling, who then sent it through the Swiss Consul's Office in China to Attie, who received the letter, on May 27, 1943, nine months after Judie died.

Attie's Return Delayed, Again

After being told several times that she would be sent to America, Attie finally realized that she would not be reunited with her family in 1942. She wrote to her family and friends in North Carolina and to Charles Maddry and M. Theron Rankin of the Southern Baptist Foreign Mission Board, letting them know that she still had no idea when she would return. Attie also described for

---

[27] Attie Bostick to Grace Stribling, contained in Attie Bostick to Miss Wang, a Chinese Bible Woman, July 15, 1942.
[28] Quoted in Edith Limer Ledbetter, "The Finest Missionary of Us All," *Royal Service,* June 1960, 38. See also ibid., 40.
[29] Bertha Bostick to Family and Friends of Judie Bostick Eskridge, August 27, 1942.

them how she spent much of her days praying, taking walks, and admiring the chrysanthemums of Mr. Wang, the Christian business manager of the hospital. Wang did his best to lift the spirits of Attie and others who remained in the hospital. Attie recounted a couple of Wang's acts of kindness: "He was there one day [while she was admiring his flowers] and said, 'Perhaps the Lord let you stay to enjoy my flowers.' I thought that was such a nice way of his putting it. He brought back many tube roses from Kaifeng when he was up there recently, and put them in pots and gave us four. This morning when I came to the sun porch it was fragrant from the two that are opening."[30]

Attie also noted in her letter that Chinese Christian friends continued to help her. Her gardener from Pochow brought a padded garment made by two Chinese women to protect her from the cold. Such a gift was helpful during the frigid winters because the internees were not allowed to purchase clothing. The members of the Baptist Sunbeams (an organization for girls under nine years of age) in Kweiteh sent a hen and thirty eggs, and a woman sent eggs and pears. Along with food and clothing, Attie also received the good news that the Pochow church continued to meet. She closed her letter with words that would not have surprised anyone: "Prices are VERY HIGH here, but we have all our needs supplied."[31]

"The Weihsien Blues"

In March 1943 Attie was among the missionaries from several denominations who, along with American and British businessmen, and college professors and administrators, were sent to the "Civilian Internment Center" in Weihsien (now Weifang), Shantung Province.[32] Attie, now sixty-seven years old, arrived at the internment center on March 22, 1943. Langdon Gilkey, a twenty-four-year-old English language teacher at Yenching University in Peking, was one of the Americans interned in Weihsien. Several years after his internment, he wrote *Shantung Compound: The Story of Men and Women Under Pressure*, in which he recounted his time at Weihsien. Gilkey explained that the Japanese did not torture or abuse the internees in the compound. What made the conditions difficult were the extreme overcrowding, the lack of sanitation during the first days of the camp, and the shortage of food and medical supplies. The Japanese crammed 1,900 people into the compound, which was a foreign mis-

---

[30] Attie Bostick to Loved Ones, Charles Maddry, and M. Theron Rankin, November 17, 1942.
[31] Ibid.
[32] See Langdon Gilkey, *Shantung Compound: The Story of Men and Women Under Pressure* (San Francisco: Harper Co., 1966), 1.

sion station the size of a city block, with the usual six-foot wall surrounding the buildings. The internees were comprised of approximately 800 people from Britain, 600 from the United States, 250 from the Netherlands, and 250 from Belgium.[33]

Gilkey, who arrived at the camp in late March, described his first impression: "The first sight that greeted us was a great crowd of dirty, unkempt, refugee-like people, standing inside the gate and coldly staring at us with resentful curiosity. Their clothes looked damp and rumpled, covered with grime and dust—much as men look who have just come off a shift on a road gang."[34] As the newcomers entered the compound, the Japanese took them to a softball field and lined them up to be counted. "For the first time," Gilkey wrote, "I noticed the guard towers at each corner or bend of the walls. I felt a slight chill as I noticed the slots for machine guns, and the electrified barbed wire that ran along the tops of the walls."[35]

The Japanese did not allow any Chinese in the compound, which meant that all of the cooking, dish washing, fire building, cleaning, clothes washing, and assistance with the daily chores fell on the shoulders of the internees. Westerners who had lived in China for any period of time had grown accustomed to the Chinese doing all of the menial work for them. For those who had never performed such tasks, life in the compound was a rude awakening.

In an attempt to keep moral high, some of the camp internees organized a theater/music group and produced musicals. Attie kept a copy of the words of one of the songs that satirized the living conditions at Weihsien—"The Weihsien Blues":

Weihsien Blues

We used to be executives, and labored with our brains,
With Secretaries neat and quick to spare us any pains.
But if the ticker tape ran out we didn't touch the thing,
The office staff could see to that, we did the ordering.
      Chorus

---

[33] Ibid, 21.
[34] Ibid, 6.
[35] Ibid, 7.

Weihsien Blues
Now we're in Weihsien, nothing's too dirty to do,
Slops, spots or garbage, or stirring a vegetable stew.
To shine in this delightful camp, you join the labor corps,

Where if you do your work too well, they work you more and more.
For since we've come to Weihsien camp, they've worked us till we're dead.
Though now we're called the labor corps, we'll be a corpse instead.

BAKER

They say that white's a color pure, so baking should be chaste,
So now you see me covered up from head to foot with paste.
But since Cordell's supporting us, the Bakery can go,
For since our Comfort money's come, why should we raise the dough.
      Chorus

BUTCHER

I used to like my steak well done; I couldn't eat it rare,
But now, when e're the cows come home, the blood gets in my hair.
We call it chops, or ribs or roast, but when the cookings through,
No matter how we cut it up, it all turns into stew.
      Chorus

STOKER

If mama just could see me now, she wouldn't know her boy,
My rosy cheeks and yellow curls were once her pride and joy,
But stoking fires and cleaning 'kwos' have crusted me with jet;
Though ladies all prefer us blonds, alas, I'm now brunette.
      Chorus

DISCIPLINE

I thought I'd take an office job to spare my lily hands,
And so I joined the camp police and issued my commands:
But when the police began to count: they put me on the shelf,
For though I counted every one I quite forgot myself.
      Chorus

LADIES

You'd think to hear those fellows sing, the men did all the work,
But I am here to tell you now the ladies do not shirk.
We clean the leeks, we cut the bread. But then what really hurts
When they have done the dirty work, we have to wash their shirts.
Chorus

(Tune—"My name is Solomon Levi.")

Attie's Letters from Weihsien

During Attie's time at Weihsien, the International Red Cross helped to re-open communication between internees and the outside world. Attie used this opportunity to write two letters from the compound. The first was a short card written to her niece Bertha on May 29, 1943, which was sent to Grace Stribling in Chengchow, who forwarded it to Bertha, who then sent it to Attie's niece Adelaide Bostick. On the card Stribling wrote the following note to Bertha: "A few minutes ago I received this card from Miss Attie. It is the first word we have had from her and of course we are very thankful to get it. Now that we know they get mail we forward, we are very happy." Attie's letter to Bertha read:

Dearest Berfy:

Yours of February telling of my dear sister's home-going, reached me through Grace and the Swiss Consul's courtesy on the 27th. I am thankful for the release from her suffering, and love to think of her as "Forever with the Lord," but it was a shock to get the word. I am so thankful Clifford [Barratt] visited you. Yes, you were right; there was no room for me on the steamship, and the second never did start. I recall dear Judie's last words to me when we kissed each other goodbye, "It is better to smile than to cry," and so after the first tears no more have come. We have been here since March 22, and are in a very nice compound, all with some work to do and happy to do it. Six of our own mission are with us, and men of all walks of life. Richard Hanson, who was a baby at TaiAn, teaches a class in Romans, another a class in John. At Easter a fine choir sang "The Crucifixion," and we have concerts weekly and some meeting nearly every night, so all are busy and happy. My love to all my friends. Letters can reach me after this, I think.

Aff'y,
Aunt Attie[36]

---

[36] Attie Bostick to Bertha Bostick, May 29, 1943. Grace Stribling received the card on July 31, 1943; Bertha received it c. October 1, 1943; Adelaide received it on October 11, 1943. On the address side of the card, the following was written: "From Miss A. T. Bostick, Civilian Center Assembly 571, 29-8, Weihsien, Shantung."

Through the Swiss Consulate in Tientsin, the U.S. State Department was negotiating with the Japanese for the release of U.S. citizens at the Weihsien compound. Attie had heard rumors that the older internees would be released first, but she had been disappointed many times before. In an undated letter probably written in August 1943 to David Yang, the Chinese Christian who was the principal of the Baptist school in Kweiteh, Attie mentioned that she had not heard from him or her other Chinese friends since she arrived at Weihsien. Her letter is scrawled on a single piece of paper. In it she prepared Yang for the reality that, once she left, she probably would never return to her beloved China:

Dear David,

Nearly 5 months have passed since we came here. Not a word from you or other friends there and at Kweiteh. Twice letters came from Misses Stribling and Murray, bringing letters from Shelby—and word my dear sister died last August—Bro. Wade [Bostick] received and appreciated your letter! God's grace has abounded and He who watches over the sparrow has abundantly cared for me. There is talk that some of us older ones will be sent to the U. S. the last of this month, but no formal notice from the authorities. It will be hard to leave the land of my adoption, but can still pray for all my friends. I do trust you and all friends there and at Kweiteh and Kaifeng are well and faithfully serving Him who gave His life for you. Christian love to all. Send [to] Stribling.

Write me. [Attie Bostick][37]

Back Home

In March 1943 the Swiss consul O. Joerg received a letter from Tomotsune Ohta of the Japanese Consulate that began the process for the repatriation of the Weihsien internees.[38] In late August 1943 Attie, along with 200 other Americans at Weihsien, began their long journey back to the United States. They boarded the Swedish ship *Gripsholm* and sailed for New York harbor.[39] The ship docked at Pier F, New Jersey, on December 1, 1943, and the headlines of the *New York Times* proclaimed:

1,400 on Gripsholm Wildly Happy Here: Reticent on Trials: Civilians freed by Japanese Burst into Song at Sight of Statue of Liberty. FBI Checks

---

[37] Attie Bostick to David Yang, c. August 1943.
[38] For details concerning the American evacuation of Weihsien, see "Agence Consularire de Sussie Tientsin" in the League, Attie T. Bostick folder, FMBCC, Box 33, SBHLA.
[39] Gilkey, *Shantung Compound*, 21.

on Arrivals, Overcrowding and Poor Food in Camps Described but Most are Healthy After Voyage. Crowded on the after promenade deck were a mass of American men, women, and children, who began to sing 'God Bless America' spontaneously when they caught their first glimpse of the Statue of Liberty on Bedloes Island. The melody was quickly taken up by those on other parts of the big vessel until it rang loud and clear across the waters of the bay.[40]

The American Red Cross brought 20,000 pounds of clothing for the internees and stretchers for those too weak to walk. Most of the former internees had gained some of the weight they had lost in the camps, and all looked tanned and happy.[41] Attie and two other missionary women rode on a Red Cross bus that took them to their designated hotel in New York City. Missionaries who had arrived earlier at the hotel gave Attie and her companions an enthusiastic welcome home![42]

During her first day in New York City, Attie met with officials from the Foreign Mission Board and with other friends. The following day, her nephew's wife met her, and after purchasing a train ticket to North Carolina, Attie, the nephew's wife, and the woman's mother all went shopping for clothes for Attie. After her trunk arrived the following day, Attie was finally able to begin the journey back to her home in North Carolina. She was overjoyed at seeing the familiar Appalachian hills, the pine trees, and the oaks. Settling back into life again in North Carolina, Attie, now sixty-eight years old, continued to live her life as a missionary. Although she could no longer minister in the "land of her adoption," she could still minister, which she did—visiting sick neighbors, folding bandages for the Red Cross, and giving talks in local churches about the mission work in China.[43]

---

[40] *New York Times*, December 2, 1943.
[41] Ibid.
[42] Attie Bostick to Mrs. Herbert, December 11, 1943
[43] Ibid.

Epilogue

She hath done what she could. (Mark 14:8)
Jesus . . . went about doing good. (Acts 10:38)

After she returned to Shelby, North Carolina, in December 1943, Attie actively supported the war and gave speeches about her work in China to local churches. Attie never forgot the people of her adopted home with whom she lived and loved in China. Just as she promised David Yang in her farewell letter to him in August 1943, Attie always remembered to pray for her friends, the Chinese Christians living in China. She officially retired from the Southern Baptist Foreign Mission Board (FMB) on October 1, 1945, at the age of seventy. Fifteen months later, on January 7, 1947, Attie, at the age of seventy-one, married Thomas Jackson (T. J.) League, an eighty-four-year-old widower, at the Bostick home on East Graham Street in Shelby.[1] Attie had met League in 1900 on the steamer while she was en route to China and League and his wife, Florence Nightingale League, were returning following their furlough to the States. League had served as a missionary in China from 1888 until 1923. He and his first wife, who died in China, had served under appointment by the FMB from 1888 to 1893, when they severed their ties with Southern Baptists in order to join the Gospel Mission program.

T. J. League and Attie Bostick, August 31, 1948

After their marriage ceremony in 1945, Attie and T. J. resided in Greenville, South Carolina. After nearly seven years of marriage, he died on December 28, 1953. Attie then moved to Forest City, North Carolina, where she lived with her

---

[1] "Retired Missionaries Are Married in Shelby; Residing in Greenville," untitled and undated newspaper clipping; Joe DePriest, "Missionaries: Bosticks devote lives to work," *Shelby Star*, December 19, 1986, 17, in the League, Attie T. Bostick folder, Foreign Mission Board Correspondence Collection (FM-BCC), Box 33, Southern Baptist Historical Library and Archives (SBHLA), Nashville, TN.

niece Bertha, who was an active member of First Baptist Church in Forest City. Attie joined First Baptist and became active there also.

In early 1965, a stroke caused Attie to move to Edgewood Rest Home.[2] Even at the rest home, the cause of missions remained foremost in her mind. According to Bertha, before Attie had to be moved to Rutherford Hospital, she asked Bertha to "write a check for $100 to the Lottie Moon offering, to which she had been giving a month's salary each year while in China."[3] Attie died at the hospital on May 7, 1965, at the age of eighty-nine.

Attie was buried holding a tattered Bible and wearing the Chinese robe she had worn many times while speaking about China to church groups. She had read the Bible through ninety-one times and had worn out several during her life.[4] Bible reading was so important to Attie that she "willed her eyes to the North Carolina Eye Bank so that 'others might see to read the Bible.'"[5] Her funeral service, which Bertha described as "a triumphant occasion," was held at First Baptist Church in Forest City, and she was buried in the Sunset Cemetery in Shelby, North Carolina.[6]

Writing from his home in Tungchow on June 17, 1891, G. P. Bostick encouraged his fifteen-year-old sister Attie to "become a very useful woman."[7] Her friend and fellow missionary Grace Stribling testified to how useful Attie became. According to Stribling, Attie "lived a rich, full and varied life as she, like the Master, went about doing good. Her placid, calm, unhurried temperament was well suited to the Chinese disposition. She had plenty of opportunities to do good and she went about doing the things that came to hand with diligence and faithfulness." Blessed with a compassionate heart, Attie used her talents and money to help the less fortunate. Although she was "frugal in personal matters," she was extremely "generous to friends and relatives, giving

---

[2] Bertha also moved with Attie into the Edgewood Rest Home, following Attie's stroke. Bertha, who had surgery in December 1963 for breast cancer, was also in declining health. She died on November 26, 1965.
[3] Bertha Bostick Bostic to Dear Friends at the Southern Baptist Convention Pension Plan, May 17, 1965. Bostic was Bertha's married name. Since 1888 Southern Baptists have held a week of prayer in December for international missions. At the end of that week, they receive a special offering for missions, called the Lottie Moon Christmas Offering.
[4] "Mrs. League, Missionary, Died Friday," *Rutherford County News*, May 12, 1965, 1; "She Was Buried in Her Chinese Robes," *Biblical Recorder*, May 29, 1965, 17, in the League, Attie T. Bostick folder, FMBCC, Box 33, SBHLA.
[5] "She Was Buried in Her Chinese Robes," *Biblical Recorder*, May 29, 1965, 17,
[6] Bertha Bostick Bostic to Dear Friends at the Southern Baptist Convention Pension Plan, May 17, 1965; James D. Marier, *The Heritage of Cleveland County* (Winston-Salem, NC: Hunter Publishing Company, 1982), 1:124.
[7] G. P. Bostick to Attie Bostick, June 17, 1891.

of time, talents and money to help and encourage."[8] Attie helped numerous young mothers care for their children. One mother expressed her gratitude to Attie, writing: "Thank you for being to us such a wonderful friend, so sweet, so sacrificial, so encouraging when we were new missionaries and needed help. You are a lovely, kind wonderful 'aunt' to all our children too. They and we are all greatly indebted to you for so much love and kindness."[9]

Just prior to leaving for China in 1889, G. P. preached a sermon titled "She hath done what she could" (Mark 14:8). During that sermon Attie heard God's call for her to be a missionary in China, and for forty-four years she remained faithful to that call. She did what she could in China and in North Carolina, and what she did in those places was "become a very useful woman."

---

[8] For Stribling's description of Attie, see Operation Baptist Biography Data Form for *Living* Person, in the League, Attie T. Bostick folder, in the Foreign Mission Board Correspondence Collection, Box 33, Southern Baptist Historical Library and Archives, Nashville, TN.
[9] Quoted ibid.

Appendix One

The Family of Samuel Evans Bostick and Jane Price Suttle[1]

Samuel Evans Bostick
(July 10, 1830-Jan. 11, 1910)

Jane Price Suttle
(Jan. 21, 1835-Oct. 23, 1921)

1. Joseph Taylor (Oct. 2, 1851- June 3, 1914)   m. Attie Hallman, Dec. 16, 1875

2. John Baxter (Mar. 30, 1853- Nov. 8, 1931)   m. Betty Durham, Aug. 25, 1879

3. Benjamin Suttle (Nov. 20, 1854-July 15, 1856)

4. William Carroll (Aug. 23, 1856- Jun. 30, 1892)   m. Mary Beam, Dec. 18, 1879

5. George Pleasant (May 29, 1858- June 21, 1926)   m. Bertha Belle Bryan, Oct. 20, 1887
m. Mary Thornton, Oct. 29, 1891
m. Lean Stover, Nov. 26, 1907

6. Sarah Louisa (Dec. 29, 1859-Nov. 28, 1922)   m. James Monroe Putnam, Aug. 4, 1881

7. Cynthia Judith (Aug. 1, 1861-Aug. 18, 1942)   m. J. D. Eskridge, Oct. 10, 1927

8. Samuel Evans, Jr. (Jan. 11, 1863-June 10, 1866)

9. Infant born dead, 1865

10. Thomas Wilkins (Sep. 16, 1866-July 23, 1867)

11. Mary Jane (Feb. 18, 1868-May 15, 1927)   m. Sam H. Austell, Mar. 20, 1888

12. Lenora Donie (Mar. 20, 1869- July 22, 1870)

13. Plato Lee (Apr. 28, 1870-Oct. 3, 1903)   m. Nettie Moore, Feb.10, 1892

14. Orlando Cephas (Jan. 5, 1872-Nov. 22, 1908)   m. Buena Hamrick, May 8, 1900

15. Wade Dobbins (Jan. 22, 1874-Sep. 24, 1944)   m. Flora Holloway, Oct. 23, 1901
m. Estelle Perry Gough, Mar. 26, 1936

16. Attie Texas (Sep. 16, 1875-May 7, 1965)   m. T. J. League, Jan. 7, 1947

17. Infant born dead, 1880

---

[1] Bertha Bostick, "Samuel Evans Bostick Genealogy," unpublished.

Appendix Two

Attie's Dates and Places of Service[1]

Dates	Place
6/1900-09/1901	Shanghai (refugee for one year)
09/1901-09/1904	Taian, Shangtung
09/1904-12/1911	Pochow, Anhwei
01/1912-05/1919	Taian, Shangtung
06/1919-01/1922	Furlough
01/1922-09/1926	Kweiteh, Honan
09/1926-04/1929	Pochow, Anhwei
04/1929-01/1931	Furlough
01/1931-10/1932	Kweiteh, Honan
10/1932-02/1938	Pochow, Honan
02/1938-10/1939	Furlough
10/1939-09/1941	Pochow, Honan
09/1941-	Kweiteh, Honan
12/1941-09/1943	Interned by Japanese

Attie's Dates of Internment

12/8/1941-01/31/1942	Lutheran compound, Kweiteh, Honan
01/31/1942-06/20/1942	Phil White residence, Kweiteh, Honan
06/20/1942-03/22/1943	Canadian Episcopal Hospital compound, Kweiteh, Honan
03/22/1943-09/19/1943	Weihsien, Shantung
09/19/1943-12/01/1943	Repatriated and arrived in U. S.

---

[1] Missionary Data Form, in the League, Attie T. Bostick folder, Foreign Mission Board Correspondence Collection, Box 33, Southern Baptist Historical Library and Archives, Nashville, TN.

Appendix Three

Conversion of Chinese Place Names

The Wade-Giles system for place names was used in the book since those were the names used at the time Attie lived in China. The current names are placed in parentheses and are based on the Pinyin system that was adopted by the People's Republic of China in 1958.

Wade-Giles	Pinyin
Anhwei	Anhui
Chefoo	Yantai
Chenhchow	Chenzhou
Honan Province	Henan
Hsuchow	Xuchang
Hwang-Hsien	Huangcheng
Kaifeng	Kaifeng
Kiang Si	Jiangxi
Kiaochow	Jiaozhou
Kuling	Lushan
Kweiteh	Shangqiu
Laichow	Laizhou
Lai Yang	Laiyang
Peking	Beijing
Pingtu	Pingdu
Pochow	Bozhou
Shanghai	Shanghai
Shansi	Shanxi
Shantung Province	Shandong
Taian	Tai'an
Tientsin	Tianjin
Tianjin Province	Tianjin Shi
Tsingtao	Qindao
Tsinan	Jinan
Tungchow	Tongzhou
Weihsien	Weifang

Index

A

Alabama Central College 14
Alexander, Mary 123
American Advisory Committee 101, 104, 111, 122
American Red Cross 131
Ann Hasseltine Missionary Society 18
Articles of Agreement 14
Asheville, NC 24
Austell, Mary 50
Austell, Sam 50
Ayers, Winnie Bennett 96

B

Barratt, Miss Clifford 83, 88, 97, 105, 110-12, 116-17, 121, 124
Barton, Laura 14
Berkley, Gerald W. 20
Blalock, T.L. 20, 29, 33, 41, 45, 54
Blalock, Mrs. T.L. 29, 33-34, 41, 45
Boiling Springs, North Carolina 10
Boiling Springs High School 48, 52
Bostick, Adelaide 10, 13, 16, 20, 23, 29, 31, 39, 40, 47, 80, 129
Bostick, Bertha Belle 10, 12-13
Bostick, Bertha May 9, 15, 28-30, 39-41, 49, 57, 64, 66, 68, 77, 95-96, 99, 101, 125, 129, 134
Bostick, Estelle Perry 86, 109, 124
Bostick, Flora 28-29, 32-35, 53, 73, 75, 80-81, 93
Bostick, George Pleasant (G.P.) 7, 9-10, 12-17, 19-20, 23, 26-29, 31, 34, 40, 47, 57-59, 71-73, 76-77, 105, 134
Bostick, Jane Price Suttle 7, 9, 12, 19-20, 25-26, 48-52
Bostick, John 7, 78
Bostick, Judie 8-9, 12, 17, 19, 24-26, 39, 48-50, 64, 66-67, 76, 86, 96-97, 99, 101-102, 105, 107, 112, 120-21, 124-25, 129-30
Bostick, Lena Stover 10, 31-32, 50, 70, 73, 77, 105
Bostick, Mary Thornton 14-16, 19-20, 26-28
Bostick, Mattie 15, 29, 31, 72
Bostick, Oreon 29, 40-41, 75
Bostick, Samuel Evans 7, 9, 12, 20, 26
Bostick, Samuel C. 16, 29, 31, 72
Bostick, Thornton 19, 29, 31
Bostick, Wade D. 7, 9, 28-29, 32-35, 39-40, 53, 59-61, 63, 71, 73-75, 78, 80, 83-84, 86, 91, 109, 110, 124, 130
Bostick, Wade H. 29, 40-41
Boxer Rebellion 7, 23-24, 26
Braun, Mary 55
Brownsboro, Kentucky 10, 13
Bryan, Stanton Pierce 13, 16

C

Canadian Episcopal Hospital 123-24
Chao, Pastor 11, 113
Chefoo 28, 43
Chenhchow 62, 100, 129
Chung, Pastor 121-123
Civilian Internment Center 126
Cleveland County, North Carolina 12, 17
Concord, North Carolina 10
Connely, Frank 53
Connely, Mary 53
Cool Springs Baptist Church 7
Cox, Addie 116

Crawford, Martha Foster 14, 19-20, 26-27, 107
Crawford, Tarleton Perry (T.P.) 14, 18-20, 26-27

D
Dawes, Joseph 53
Dawes, Laura 40, 47, 53
Ditminson 115-116, 119, 121-22, 124
Ditminson, Mrs. 115-116
Dong, Pastor 70-71, 73

E
Empress Dowager 23

F
Feng, Yu Hsiang 66, 71
First Baptist Church, Durham, North Carolina 10
First Baptist Church, Forest City, North Carolina 134
First Baptist Church, Gastonia, North Carolina 19, 37, 42, 93
Floyd's Creek, North Carolina 7, 10, 26
Flynt, Wayne 20
Ford, Jessie 101-03, 108
Foreign Mission Board (FMB) 12, 14, 19, 32-35, 39, 41-46, 48, 51-53, 55, 59, 62-63, 68, 77-7, 81, 84-86, 88, 96-97, 100, 102, 108, 125, 131, 133
Forest City, North Carolina 7-8, 133-34

G
Gastonia, North Carolina 18
Gilkey, Langdon 126-127
Gospel Mission 18, 20, 26, 29, 33, 35, 37, 39, 41-42, 44-45, 54-55, 133
Greenville, South Carolina 133

Gripsholm 130

H
Harris, Florence Powell 100
Herring, David W. 19-20, 26-27
Honan 53, 57, 62, 66, 71
Honan-Anhwei Baptist Association 69
Hsin, Pien Hsiang 121
Hsu 121
Hsuchow 71-72
Huggins, J.D. 52
Hylbert, L.C. 111-112, 122
Hwang-Hsien 46, 62

I
International Red Cross 129

J
Japan 94-95, 102, 110-111, 115
Japanese 94, 96-97, 99-100, 105, 108-13, 115, 117, 121-23, 126-27, 130
Joerg, O. 130
Jiangxi 80
Jones Seminary 17
Judson, Adoniram 17
Judson, Ann Hasseltine 17
Judson College 17-18, 78, 80
Judson Conversationalist 18

K
Kaifeng 53, 58-59, 62, 65-73, 79, 100, 103, 113, 116, 123, 126, 130
Kelly, Willie 18, 24
Kelsey, Nurse 115-16, 119, 123-24
Kiaochow 46
Kih, Fang Long 65
King, Harriett 83, 86, 89, 97-99, 105
King, Mary 69, 89, 99-100, 105
King, W.D. 19-20, 26-27

Knight, Fannie 14, 20
Kuling 80, 82
Kweiteh 53, 58-59, 62, 65-73, 77-80, 98, 103-04, 110-11, 113, 115-16, 119, 121-24, 126, 130

L

Laichow 46
Lai Yung 46
Lawton, Deaver 62
Lawton, Dorothy 62
Lawton, Mary 62-63
League, Florence N. 14, 19-20, 25-27, 40, 55-56, 133
League, Thomas J. 14, 19-20, 25-27, 40, 55-56, 133
Li, Chang K'ai 98
Louisville, Kentucky 10, 47
Love, J. Franklin 52-55, 58
Lutheran Compound 115-116, 120-121

M

Maddry, Charles 84-86, 93, 97, 100, 104, 109-10, 113-15, 125
Marion, Alabama 17-18
Meredith College 28
Ming, Dong Si 65
Moon, Lottie 14, 35
Moore, J.D. 93
Murray, Katie 116, 125, 130

N

Nashville, Tennessee 31-32

O

Ohta, Tomotsune 130

P

Pearl Harbor, Hawaii 114-15

Peking 12, 40, 63, 111
Pingtu 14, 46
Pochow 27-29, 31-35, 47, 57-59, 62-63, 69, 73-76, 80-83, 86, 88, 90, 95, 96-101, 103-05, 111, 113, 116, 121, 123, 126, 134
Poteat, Gordon 844-85
Prosser, Lois 86, 110-12, 116, 110,121
Pruitt, Anna 14
Pruitt, C.W. 14
Putnam, Louisa (Lou) 8, 50

Q

Qing dynasty 23, 66
Qinghua University 24

R

Raleigh, North Carolina 10, 28
Rankin, M. Theron 102, 125
Ray, T. Bronson 42-48, 50, 62-63, 84
Ren, Lao Yang 66
Riddell, Olive 74-76, 92, 110
Ridgecrest Baptist Assembly 99
Rutherford County, North Carolina 7, 9, 12, 26

S

Sallee, Hannah 116
Sallie, Annie Jenkins 33, 71
Shanghai 7, 12-13, 23-24, 73-74, 84-86, 91, 107, 111, 113, 122-23
Shansi 23
Shantung Province 19-20, 23, 26, 47, 54, 62, 74, 112, 126
Shelby, North Carolina 7-9, 16-17, 24, 48, 80, 97, 122, 130, 133-34
Southern Baptist Theological Seminary 10
Southern Baptists 14, 26, 33, 85, 101
Sheppard, Susie V. 14-15

Smythwick, Gladys 99-100
Stribling, Grace 74, 100, 110, 112, 116, 125, 129-30, 134
Strother, Greene 76, 83, 88-91, 93, 97-98, 101, 105, 109-10
Strother, Martha 83, 86, 89-91, 97, 105, 108-10
Su, Mrs. 112-13
Suttle, B.F. 50
Suttle, J.W. 52
Swiss Consul Office 125, 129-30

T

Taian 19-20, 26-27, 34, 41-42, 46-47, 51-55, 57, 73, 129
Tai- Shan 46-47, 55
Taoist 46
Thornton, J.G. 15
Tientsin 72, 130
Townshend, Sarah 45-46, 53, 58, 67, 69-71, 77-78
Townshend, Sidney 46, 53, 58, 67, 69-71, 77-79
Tsinan 72
Tsingtao 74
Tung 59
Tsining 53, 74
Tungchow 12, 14-15, 17, 46
Tuscaloosa, Alabama 14

U

U.S. State Department 130

W

Wake Forest College 10, 28
Ward, Josephine 116
Walker, Blanche 61
Weihsien 126-30
Wen 82
White, Mattie Macon 70, 74, 98, 103, 106, 110
White, Phillip 70, 74, 98, 103, 106, 110-11, 113, 119, 121-23
Willingham, Robert J. 33-35, 51-52
Woman's Missionary Union 79, 122

Y

Yang, David 112-13, 121, 130, 133
Yu Xian 23
Yuan, Shiki 66

Z

Zoar Baptist Church 8